Ballroom
Lyn Lifshin

FOREWORD

I love these poems. I enjoyed reading them immensely. What comes across in them is strong and clear and passionate, as the dance must be if it's to be a success. Your longing is appropriately ironic and sweet by turns, and the imagery is fluid, again like the dance. The poems are charming and funny, but definitely not light fare. I think some of your best work to date can be found in this collection. The descriptions of the dances are spot-on, visceral, and strikingly visual at times, like dancers illuminated by flashes of light, caught in provocative poses, in flourishes of festive colors. I thought of Bruegel. I thought of Dr. Williams' *Pictures from Bruegel* wherein the dancers go round/they go round and round reminding us how fundamental dance is to the human experience. As is poetry. In these poems you found the best words to exemplify the wordless phenomena of dance, to convey the experience of the dancer sensually, always on the brink, but never quite reaching full abandon.

Lyn Lifshin keeps rejuvenating herself defiantly against all the odds of the game, through one batch of poems after another, dancing, as in the case of these poems, gracefully and provocatively, a few quick steps ahead of the inevitable shadow pursuing us all. The poems are interwoven with recordings of dreams that complement the dance-poems to strangely assymetrical effect. The lines are as diligently rendered and as apparently the product of physical abandon as are the variable thrusts and parries of the ballroom dances that inform these poems each step of the way.

The moves of the dancers are brought back to life on the page under Lifshin's probing touch. At times it's as if the words can barely keep up with the tempo of thought being driven by the dance. All of it is tied into a larger theme that encompasses a lifetime of desire and loss, humor and lassitude. The dance says it all, beautifully, and brutally when necessary, and in these formidable poems it drives the intent of the poet home again and again spinning breathlessly until we get it right.   —Joe La Rosa

I

Ballroom

SOMETIMES BEFORE SLEEP

it's like tuning into
distant stations. Or
an SOS alert, indelible
as lips or skin. Call
it ESP. If I didn't shudder,
your tango moving
toward me like a
brand, each place your
fingers touched,
indelible, a stain I
can't let fade

WHEN YOU TURN
CHA CHA
INTO A MAD GIRL
POEM

and I didn't plan to do it.
When this dangerous tango
slams me from despair
to a five-margarita high,
to look back would be a
guillotine. When no rumba
is torture, when all that
matters, all that is real is
fantasy. Just your eyes and
the v in my bikini is soaking.
I can barely imagine
surviving anything more
invasive. Each deep look
a bruise that doesn't fade

WHEN
THERE ARE MARIACHIS

when breakfast and lunch
are martinis. When
sheets smell of rose,
Bulgarian rose, Tuber
rose, that dark rose
in a bottle on my dresser,
musky as skin. When
it's bolero or rumba.
When we leave the
room, and there is no
cat puke to clean up,
no terror of what's
ahead. When you hold
me, should you hold me

YOUR EYES
IN THE CROWDED
ROOM

I'm in for it
now, not that longing
isn't what I wanted,
feeling that alive

No wonder I'm not
the only one sure
it's you. Their skin's
been torched.

I'm stunned by the
day's tattoo where
your fingers held me

SEXY IS GOOD AS IS OBAMA

he said you got to put
the two together. That
inauguration poem
didn't do it: my ball
room teacher, a man
who ought to know.
He loves Obama,
moves as he moves,
eyes on a point you
know he's going to
get to, moving smooth,
moving with grace.
I think of a panther or
lynx slivering thru
brush and tall grass
with ease, riveting,
they seem to flow,
stealthy, muscles
rippling, taking you
along with them, sure
they are going to be
worth the way they
keep you shivering,
how your heart pounds

THE I GO BACK TO SCHOOL DREAM

of course I'm older than the other students.
My mother and father, back from under the
earth, drive me to the campus. I'm sure I'll
never find my way around. The room is
Spartan, small desk, dresser I can't imagine
the few things I've brought with me will fit.
Already I feel I don't fit, keep misplacing
the key. When I see two beds, I realize
I'm going to have a room mate. I don't think
this will work. No space, no air around me.
And of course I have the wrong clothes. By
chance, I meet a woman outside in the light.
She's pretty and very sweet. She says she is
Japanese but I'd never know. In the next
frame, there's a modern dance class in my room.
I need the exercise but there are feet every
where, trampling over the leather jacket I
threw over the desk. I don't know about this,
I like dance but the other students are leaving
their Big Mac wrappers on the floors that
weren't too clean anyway and where is my cat,
Jetè? She shouldn't be able to wander, would
never survive on the street and I want to phone,
phone any one but I don't have my cell phone
and there's not a phone booth on campus.
My room mate, seeing the crowd, has now it
seems taken the bed and moved into a new
room. That is a relief I think on my hands
and knees scrubbing the floor. My cat safe
inside on the window ledge and tho some burly
man has rubbed up against me and tried to put
his hand between my legs, he's gone, there
I am a la Lady Mac Beth, still frazzled, trying
to convince myself there is nothing wrong with
just wanting out

ON THE STALLED METRO

on my way to ballet,
wild to dance the
voodoo wild blues
out of me while he
dreams of Audrey
Tautou and Javier
Bardem. He is
forgetting my words,
the poems he
remembered longer
than many. What
can you expect from
a man who wanted
to collect stones
and be a zoo keeper,
cage animals, paint
and trap what once
was free, to have
them, like all the
women who trail him,
caught for him in
case he's in
the mood

WHERE WILL PASSION
TAKE YOU?
ON THE METRO TO DC.
OR THE DREAM FINALLY
OF THE MAN I CAN'T HAVE

it's not that I haven't wanted him,
tried at least to hold him
in a dream. He has a wife, and
then, there's the significant other.
"Don't crash," some one warned
me. Obsession. Yes but he is
only mine in poems. But last night,
it was, after not able to sleep,
I checked email and Face Book.
His warmest child hood memory
the same as mine, his words
enticing as his dancing. Then
later, he was suddenly there,
with me, in a cottage with a pool
and sun so unlike the last dark
weeks. I relaxed in pale dotted
Swiss, feel easy as I often don't
waltzing into the ballroom,
dreading the young beauties
always a circle of them around
him, better dancers than I
am, their beautiful arms in
halter tops but for this moment
I'm suspended, nothing in this
frame doesn't glow. He is in
shade. I can only a part of
his body, coal hair glistening.
Alone in this perfect get-away.
A little more perfume and
since he loves them, a martini
as I lean closer, let what's
about to happen happen

I CAN BARELY
CONCENTRATE
ON THE STEPS,
HIS EYES, HIS LIPS
MYSTERIOUS
AS THE LIPS OF HORSES

there was that poem he
says, the one, you know
Juarez and the porch.
It's volcanic, it's a
different language.
It's code. This isn't
Austin after too many
margaritas. Do you think
I want it to be? Want
you to want me? Be
the leather jacket another
picked up and carried
gently? When you
say "you fascinate, you
are invention," I'm
astonished. I'm the addict
I knifed my way from
being. When you're
a drug, a dangerous
rumba no one comes
back from with what they
had. And your words
pelt, a tattoo, a brand.
I'm dazed. It's not the swirl
of the dance spinning
and I know if I don't wake
up this could play
out as you said
and you know I am gold

11

THE SICKENING DREAM OF BEING FROZEN
ON THE BLEACHERS, MUCH LIKE A

hooker waiting to do
what some man requests.
It goes back to high
school. 7 PM to mid
night just sitting,
waiting, never
guessing nobody
would ask me to
dance. A brand, a
tattoo, it's a needle
in my blood,
indelible. Sure I
got all A's and won
the science and
art contests but none
of that mattered, sitting
in stupid decorated
socks while girls
who went across the
state line to
pet and drink in
back seats were swept
up, went swirling.
Even now with more
lovers than I can count,
sitting in a half
dark room with a
drivel of short men
who have the
choice of at least 12
babes, most of
them in their 20's,
I'm flung back like

last night when
the one I came with
began horsing around
and diddling with
baby Asians while I
was abandoned,
staggering from the
center of a foot
ball sized dance floor
where anyone
who wasn't decrepit
was taken, twenty year
olds with their pony tails
flapping like corn tassels,
galloping past the field.
There's mud on my
shoes—to hell with
sticking with the one
who brought me. He's
gone to who knows where.
I don't know why they
didn't at least mow
the grass, blades
like knifes. The sun
getting hotter, like a
fair grounds. He can be
miles away but I'm
not hot footing it thru
rubble and you can just
guess, wild and raging
as my heart feels,
just where I am aiming for

the men, there aren't enough.
So the women wait,
wall flowers, Cinderellas
pretending it is ok. I
think it is humiliating. I
did this in high school,
my pasted on fake smile.
I hate it. The men, there
aren't enough of them
and the ones that are there,
excuse me, some things
are better left unsaid.
It must be like this at a
beauty pageant or a
whore house. Will my
rose perfume attract
the right one? It must be
as humiliating at a beauty
contest or a brothel.
Tits and ass, the old
story. Even the most
beautiful at bolero
are like girls at a bar,
pretending to talk to
each other as they wait.
Most can't pull it off.

Even the ones who look
gorgeous in the right
man's arms, have to
put up with clods,
begin to think they
ought to be at home
reading a good book. If
it was a dream, then
I'd want to wake up.
Even the beauties you'd
hold your breath over
are out-numbered. I
will never not remember
waiting a whole night
in decorated socks
and no one walked
over to me. I will never
not be that 14 year old
old maid. Sure I'm
camouflaged in beautiful
clothes
and when someone who
matters pulls me into tango
my silk swirls but I
am shadow

NIGHTMARE THAT WAS WORSE THAN ANY NIGHTMARE DREAM

as if the worst thing I
could imagine happen
and it happened. Right
there. I walked into the
room and just seeing
her I wanted to grab
my keys, turn the dream
into a film run back
wards. First one foot
even tho I was frozen, a
deer in the car lights
doom, then the other.
I wanted to be back in
my own rooms, wanted
to peal off the red silk
dress but she was
there in his arms, the
dance floor a mine
field. Then, in the glare,
it was their silhouettes.
But I saw him lean
toward the side of her,
a plunge to her cheek,
and then her hand slammed
up to slap him. Whatever
wasn't ruined inside me
might as well have
been. That sting, and
the rest of the night, the
bruise spreading. One
mark on top of another.
In the kitchen the

food made me sick.
Then when he weirdly
held on to my hand.
Or when he touched me,
grabbed me, then walked
by and didn't ask me
to dance. A relief this
time as, drunk and drugged,
he grabbed other women
to kiss. He danced samba
so wildly, as if dark spirits
were in him, one slip and
it would be the perfect
storm. I smiled
thru other men's
fingers, thought of
Elizabeth Edwards
saying that she threw
up hearing her news.
The night couldn't
have ended soon enough.
Each dance torture,
each glance his way
and I wanted to what?
kill or cry? How I still
slept that night is a
mystery. How I didn't
realize until morning
what sickened me so
was what he did to her
wasn't to me

THE WAY TO BALLROOM,
PRIVATE MONDAY LESSONS

to be held. I don't need
a white close- to- strapless
dress but the arms of
someone who knows what
he's doing. Don't let
Obama's be a one night
dream of gliding and
flowing, let him hold us
close with style, let us
move not like some clod
who steps all over you,
jerks you one way then
yanks you out of yourself,
leaves a heap of what's
left of you on the floor

TANGO WITH HIM
AND HE LEAVES A STAIN

it's indelible,
he's glued to your skin.
Then, that staccato
pull away that leaves
dark skid marks.
"dumped by," I
want to say his name
but it ought to be
on t shirts, a warning,
revenge. He'll hold
you so close you
can't breathe, leave
you panting with no
thing but dark
indigo. Each scar a
Rorschach he was
wild for, then
tossed. In love with
the chase, a hunter, he
sees what he wants
thru the cross
hairs. He uses his
charm like a
gun. He's a dancer
who can turn. He
moves into you with
his eyes, his
bolero. Everywhere
he was you are
not what
you were

HE ONLY WANTS WHAT CAN'T LAST LONG, LIKE THE AIR BEFORE IT RAINS

to him, you're the deer
he's on the prowl for
with bones hot and
gorgeous as flamenco.
Once he's got you
he loses interest, it's
all in the chase.
What he adores, lusts
for and worships,
changes fast as his
profile picture
on Face Book. What
he's wilder for than he
can sputter begins
to bore, spread
eagle on his desk:
a book, a woman, carne
quisda con queso. He
wanted to paint but

he was too busy
chasing babes. His bad
boy act is not resistible
and reels them in. It's
always like the
tango he teaches, a
yank wildly in
so you'd merge with
his body and
then you're thrown out,
flung away with a
wild heel stamp,
staccato. Tho once
he was in love
with her he abandoned
Cyd Charrise as he
will you for a
young version, say
Isabelle Huppert

WHEN THERE'S
NO GOOD TANGO

When you need a
little more staccato,
when it's one step
after another, no
fire, no pizzazz. When
the love-hate fizz
is gone, no wild
lure, no La Cucaracha
in the sheets, over
a no candle dinner,
a cold potatoes and
squash mood, a no
twists a no come
hither, no attitude,
no swirls and swivels,
no dazzling poetry of
hips. It just snows
and drizzles three
weeks straight,
over coats instead
of flaming colors slit
up the thigh, way
past the Buenos Aires

WITH HIM IT WAS
NO ZESTY TANGO

Nothing slow with a
sudden shot of spice.
No swivels, no soft
rock in a hot mango
breeze. Just, honey,
give me a rock step
into you know where,
baby, I'm waiting to
be pulled in. I've
softened my knees,
my hips are saying
what my lips won't
pressed up against a
hip. Bodies should
be blending, a dip
then a promenade.
Wild love and hate.
Staccato. Uncurl me,
throw me out and
then pull me reckless-
lessly back again

THE TROT

Foxy, that was what
men yelled that
other December,
Muscle Beach. Was
it my fox jacket?
The mini? Or just
being out in the dark?
Those old reading
series charades,
pretending to be
foxy, needing to be
foxy, a babe those
years few women said
the words I did,
shaking inside. I
must have run out for
booze to be smooth,
to be sure. On the
beat, moving, gliding
over panic like pro
dancers in a fox trot.
Foxy. How little
I was like that. Vodka, a
camouflage gliding
Into beds as easy as the
beat

SAMBA SOME DAYS

Pull me in
and toss me away as
long as the music's
going. I'm that girl
in Buenos Aires,
swiveling hips, a big
jangly head dress,
glass chunks the
moon spits into
the night. Rubies,
sapphire and emerald
and hardly anything
else. My rollicking
strut will make
nipples blur like
tigers turning to butter
or the lines in a pin
wheel. My hips
a snake I think you'd
be almost afraid
to touch

BOLERO

that dip toward you
like a heron going
for the glint of
fish and them I'm
backing away. A
little somnambulistic
sway. Who can
decide if they want
to go forward or
backward. Smooth,
you'e smooth baby,
I could drift in
your arms. The
waves of the body,
and then we
cross over. What
arms could do

AFTER A DAY LIKE TODAY

I need what's smooth, a
lift, what will lift up

my long hair and roll it
into a chignon, like

grief, a shot, a heel to
ball, a little Sinatra

not a "hop" and "hup,"
into staccato tango

or swing. But a strong
still gentle rib to rib,

this sweep over the
polished floor. Any

thing uneasy, braided
into a grapevine,

everything smooth
as rhinestones or

velvet, the night
a double twinkle

ROOMBAH, YES?

the Russian teacher grins.
We do Latin tonight,
yes? Her face, candles
from a city close to
Mosow. Fans and spiral
swivels. The dance
floor's icy wood melts
under her giggle. The
beat is coming, the
heat is coming. What
wasn't done in the office
and should have been
blurs like the edges
of the room, fanning and
swirling. My body lifts
upward, my knees soften
like those parts that let
existence begin

RUMBA

no matter icycles
are glazing doors

when the rhumba
music starts to play,

starts the sway,
only your body

a touch, a dip,
the knees soften.

Give me a Spanish
comb, a flame

swirl, skin and
rock back to snap

in your body, your
eyes. Let me go,

let my hips lure
you and then

spiral me and let
me look deep

THE WET GRASS UP PAST MY CALVES DREAM

I'm at a conference, kind of like AWP only
dancers, like David, a kind of kidding
around teddy bear of a man. We are at
tables signing books. Now I wish I'd told
him his name was the title of the first poem
I published. But no mater, maybe then he
wasn't even born. Tho I don't have a book,
I know I ought to do networking. Even
the word seems grey, a day with no color,
no sky. Then I see a man who used to always
invite me to be poet in residence tho the
last two years, suddenly only silence. I wrote
him, I e mailed. But he's here tho some
how very nasty. There's another much closer
friend but I need to get out fast. My car is
in underground parking and it's getting
late but when I try to find my car, the exits
go nowhere. It's a labyrinth, a maze with no
way to escape. I ditch my car. Next thing
I'm walking in rain, the wet grass up
past my calves and no Rapunzel, no prince,
no one, nothing in the rain to save me

BALLROOM, BLUE

so this is how it
feels, the floor tilting
where we locked in a tango

slipping away as
someone changes the cd

what was ghostly as
strains going under

with the Titanic.
How could I know I was
stuck on
an iceberg

under all the show, the glitz?

How could I hear
signs of distress. How could
I not believe it was

really happening.
Or expect to survive

What was it, your
moon light sea eyes
that paralyzed?

BALL ROOM GIGOLOS
AND THE JEWELED
AND POWDERED LADIES

at the competition, the men are
all studs, their posture is perfect.
In their rhinestone swirls, the
women's stockinged legs glisten.
Years past being cougars, their diamonds glare,
hide their skin

In their rhinestones, swirling, these women
won't place an ad for a companion or go to
church socials.
Like a last gasp, they've nothing to lose.
Better to dance towards death in the
arms of a gorgeous man.
What does it matter if they have to pay for it?

Like a last gasp, they tango with
all the fire left.
If flesh isn't the flesh it was
it's still flesh.
What better to dipped, be held by a lady
killer man, even if only for hours?
What better than a player, a seductive partner
not likely to die or need 24/7 care?

If their flesh isn't what it was, the
gowns dazzle. What young girl could afford
$ 4,500 for a beaded rhinestone dress,
hotel and air. These men sparkle but they
will burn out like a star.

The ball gowns dazzle as if they will
scare death away.
Most have never seen such beauty
or such beautiful men except their grand children.
Some took care of a sick man.
Now it's their turn.

So many women never saw such
beauty. The gowns, the ballroom,
the men. A breath and the bolero is
over fast as beauty, as life

The gowns, the ballroom, the men,
they look invulnerable, intoxicating
as what is on a movie screen.
In the whirl of silk what is blurs

GIGOLO BALLROOM

only the ball gowns are lovely,
$4,500 for gold and sequins
and silk, a little less for a
black tulip floating over
rose petals. Once these women
were as young as these studs,
the young male dancers.
Trapped in suburban kitchens
maybe or waiting for some
man to come back from
war to run into offices where
their young secretaries played
at adoring them or did. Now,
it's the women's turn. Some
still slim, some with chiseled
cheek bones. But all with
enough money now that it's
their time to play. Why check
the personals for a man their
age probably looking for a
nurse or a woman who will drive
them to doctors or early bird
dinners when a handsome
ballroom dude, gorgeous often
and trying to please can whisk
them off to Las Vegas, smile
with adoration as they compete
before the ballroom dancing

judge and gallantly drop them
off at their room. No fuss no
muss while he goes off to get
drunk and do a little karaoke.
The women need their beauty
sleep, might or might not think
of dead husbands, know they can
play the dance field as long
as they can pay. The delicious
boy toys can't afford to escape
with the young beauties they'd
chose. And much as they love
the foxtrot, Stepping Out and
the swing's Spin a While, for
them, too, it will only be
a while

THE CHAMELEON

Some days he's the sheik, he's
Valentino, slicked back hair
for a dangerous tango. A
day later it's jeans, the bad
boy, the hipster. His sneer
pierces. His beard grows in
over night. Some days he's
French, some days Italian.
He's the sheik in more ways
than one. The heart breaker,
the Valentino. Tango with
him and he leaves a stain.
One day he'll bring you
chocolate, another he's in his
Fred Astaire hat, is the dance
away lover. Too many women
linger near his tent. Valentino
in a pale striped summer
suit, Valentino in the tuxedo.
The days he's Viennese,
your feet won't touch the
ground. He smells sweet as
he says you do. For beat or
hippy days, his sweat smells,
thrills some. If death gets
him young like Valentino,
the train with his gorgeous corpse
would stall traffic. Long haired
girls, blue as the silver bloom,
or the tart and sweet blueberry
will cry and no one no one will
know who he went out as

WHEN YOU ARE WITH THE CHAMELON
YOU NEVER KNOW WHO YOU ARE

one day you are Pola Negri
to his Valentino. You trail
the white roses she brought
to his grave. On Tuesday
he's the irresistible bad boy,
oily black hair and a wake of
Asian beauties drooling,
falling all over him. You
feel you're too pale and of
course not even a babe.
When he wears his gangster
shoes, he won't hug but
he'll make you shiver.
When he wears a top hat,
a la Fred Astaire you know
it's a day he needs more
to feel hunky, feel special.
Maybe his baby cried.
Maybe he didn't like how
his wife nagged or maybe
he didn't score high on the
competition. Maybe, alone,
on his own, he didn't score.

With him you don't know
if it's the day he's daddy
to a young Cambodian
girl or feels so poor he
wants a sugar Mama.
On Face Book he's a
pirate, a rooster, a witch.
Some days he's his suave
self or maybe a porcupine.
Some days he's his beautiful
innocent child and then
or course there are days
he's the devil. Where you
stand is like particles of
glass in a kaleidoscope,
shifting and never the same.
You feel jagged, tossed
around as those little jewel
pieces, never sure except
that you stay glued to
what keeps changing,
startling and eerie longer
than you should

SCARS

that one shaped like a 7. Bryant Park,
the first slit in skin you could see
shaped like a 7. It was at the close
of a reading and I wasn't ready to give
up my mic for a talk by Governor
Rockefeller. In the bar I saw blood
soaking thru my wedgewood blue
long dress, stuck to my skin
from where what they pulled from
me boomeranged. I shortened the
dress 12 inches. Then I was scalped,
or nearly. I wasn't in any war, just on
the way to meet a friend for a film.
I suppose it was poetry that did
me in: I was mailing some ms when
the car behind me slammed into
the car right ahead into a car coming
from the opposite direction. 250
stitches and my amethyst barrette.
Gone. Mummy wrapped. And I adored
that orchid stone. But it wasn't until
the white gauze came off and I could see
the jabbed barbwire. I shuddered
at what looked like a knife falling
from the space I was sunbathing under.
That scar seemed to glow in the bed
room when we turned out the light.
Now I wear my hair over the slash, may
be why I slammed wildly, into the treacherous,
sharp slate steps and hacked my shin to
the bone. A machete chop on top of
where a suitcase falling made a blood
trail thru the house, bled thru gauze
12 days. Blood poured thru another hall
as skin torn as if sawed, flowed. The

towel couldn't stop it. The stitches a scar
on top of a scar, a criss cross, rail
road tracks, a gas explosion. More months
of bandages, salves, adhesives, silver
and adaptic. No tights, no stockings no
mini skirts, no ballet, not even ballroom.
No skin that looks or feels like skin again
like when you slid out of my arms

DREAM OF WHEN I COULD NO LONGER

imagine his pierced tongue,
how "Tainted Sequins"
could be those fantasies,
glittery, but ruined,
not a film, not a dress
with copper flares.
When I could no longer
pretend our bodies
pressed in close, *closer*
he said, his hips against
my hips, *roll them in*,
closer meant anything more
than a position for tango.
When our legs were
touching, deeper he said
my thighs burning. It
was only technique. He
had more women
then he could deal with.

How does anyone stay
together he whispered,
his mouth on my ear,
his thigh fire. My
skin was burning. I
thought of another hunk
women drooled for
when we walked under
dripping eucalyptus, before
I was no longer my verbs,
I was no longer the
lure, my legs a drug, a
challenge he couldn't resist,
a wildness. And how long
could he stare at the me
in the monitor, how long
could he lick my poems as
if they were skin of a
ballroom of beauties all
aching for him

WHEN HE SAID
YOU'RE SHOWING SOME SKIN

when a boat neck velvet slipped
an inch off my shoulder.
Skin. His fingers holding,
When I wasn't scared
I couldn't follow. Who knows
if it was a night I
couldn't sleep, if more than
his touch was throbbing.
Slant light, the wild cherries opening.
When he bent me, bent me
in places I never thought
I could go, over, water in his
arms. When I wasn't thinking, just
trusted him. Then the waltz
stopped

WHAT I WANT

you try a few dances with
a few of the better men,
bolero or waltz, see
how they measure
up. I like the slow
dances best, like
dating, making love,
making a poem
that jolts or makes
somebody giggle.
At some point
I decide who I
like best (ok, I
won't pretend, esp.
on paper I
haven't) and then
I want to dance like
having mind blowing,
irresponsible
condom-less sex,
imagine like
Li Po there is
no end to things

INSOMNIA

when not even the
7th rerun of Dancing
with the Stars
doesn't do it and
hot milk just makes
a dirty cup. When
valium isn't helping
and ambien makes
me feel odd. When
codeine makes me
dazed the next
day, as if I was
with you

BE AFRAID, VERY

The dance poems he asks.
At least I think that's
how he put it. This close,
I go into an altered state.
Should I be afraid?
he asks and I laugh,
*very. And then some you
will love.* He comes back
at me with the blackest
eyes, chameleon, each
part more hypnotic.
These poems are like
enormous boobs lately so
many are sporting,
toppling from low cut
dresses or the scent French
women dab behind their
ears, eau de vagina.
One dab and men go wild.
These poems, like a
bare midriff jeans slice
from, like a petticoat
in the old days, maybe
something like a burka
only the eyes burn
from luring men to
imagine, ache for what
in their imagination is
so much more than they
could be

BECOMING
WHAT YOU'RE CALLED

some nights, lets say
last night, halfway across
the dance floor could
have been Ethiopia,
the moon. Until I was
wine an alcoholic
drooled for,
chocolate some
diabetic couldn't
refuse. No matter I
am not the beauty I
might have been, the
dancer no one
can resist. Those
poems about ballroom
could be marijuana,
someone he once
dreamed of on a night
of crack. Some one
he's a little wary of,
a little unsure but
nothing intrigues
him now

THE STACCATO
OF HIS EYE

something animal
wild to spring,
the dream sweep
then the world
chase. That snap,
red silk the
onyx tango that
isn't for the sky,
a blood tango,
knife the breaks,
always the edge
slivering close.
Sometimes I am the
red shoes
vixen asked "do you
want to live?" she
was poised to leap,
she was something in
me suspended in
arms, the pounding
the deepest. Asked
do you want to
live, wind from the
metro tunnel, a
lover, in tango,
always the red shoes.
Did she want to live?
She had to dance

SOMETIMES IT'S LIKE

the child dancing in
the Warsaw ghetto
in his body of rags

there must have been
music no one
could hear

dancing thru corpses,
his face pale as the moon
just to stay alive,

begging *please
don't hurt me.* Dancing
to horror. No one

could hear what
he heard, the razor's
edge, the body's language

WALTZ

where you're someone else,
the drawn to flame moth daze.
The world goes away.
This trance deeper than drugs.
Don't imagine anyone could hold me.
I'm flame, wings, a heartbeat
could shatter. Something moves in
under skin, something that
could turn me into Isadora, oblivious
to rain and snow. In the right
arms, I'm wind, rain and fire,
wild to be held tight as
Isadora, to be wound around
skin, your skin, your fingers a
ride in the flame scarf wrapping her
tight and tighter

TAKE A BROOMSTICK
TO THE NEXT BALLROOM CLASS

not because you're witchy. Oh forget anyone
who scowls "the newbies have to learn too."
Look, when you've been paying big bucks,
sometimes on the metro lulled in a trance you
could image floating over the rails, chiffon
and your head bent back not as if your partner
had bad breath but as if your neck was swan
gorgeous, your back perfect. You own the floor
and of course there's a prince leading so well
even if you don't believe you'll ever learn
to follow brilliantly, after all in how many ways
have you ever? But between Falls Church and
Foggy Bottom—you're a sprite in 5 inch heels.
The music is more deep in you than any man.
Then the train jolts to a screech. If this wasn't
fantasy and you were really in those smashing
gold heels you'd probably have a concussion
toppling into the subway's metal bar
but you grab your back pack and in moments
are in the chilly studio. Except you've forgotten,
instead of a suave or even demi suave dancer
from say Dancing with the Stars, there's a
slew of let's be honest: not at all hunky men who
would stumble, sober, walking an intoxication
test. They step on your toe or slam you into
another clod. Lucky if your toes aren't blue,
your ring finger matching it so I say girl,
since you'll never find a prince in the low level
class who can sweep you off the floor take my
advice, bring your broom

IF YOU DON'T
GIVE IN, HE
WON'T DANCE

with you. Withhold,
and he'll withhold.
It's not your body
he of course really
wants. I mean "my"
body. He might want
yours. It's the body
of my work. Oh
forget the horse
poems, the ones
about mothers and
daughters. Ballroom
poems are what he
wants. He's wild,
he's excited. He says
he's a little scared,
looks at me with
eyes no one living
could get over.
"Should I be scared?"
he grins? I'm on
the verge of giving in,
giving him any
thing he wanted. He's
always wanted what
he wanted until he
got it and what
he wants most is
what I have and won't
give up to him

HE WANTS
WHAT HE CAN'T HAVE

He wants it until
he has it. He's not
unique in longing for
the chase. What's elusive
has its own iridescence.
Whether love or lust
lasts, it can't stay
what he lusts for.
Excited, terrified, he
has to have what
only I can make in poems.
Maybe he's scared
I know him too
well tho I haven't even
been with him. What
I make will last longer than
his passion. He knows
what I've done with
other lovers. He knows how
once I've touched them,
do what I've done
to them, neither of us
will be the same

HE'S ON HIS KNEES

you might think
he was begging,
maybe he is but
it's not my body
he's after. Others
have been but
no mind. He wants
what's deeper in.
Don't think he's
a saint, think
instead Narcissus.
He won't dance
with me until I give
in. He won't look
at me lately. He's
waiting for an
e mail poem. One
women said he
was magic, talked
of his soul, his beauty.
I can't say I don't
find him irresistible
and do you think
I like that? And that
he won't ask me
to dance

"SHOULD I BE SCARED? I'M EXCITED,
A LITTLE WORRIED"

I smile, my flirtatiousness, a mask, camouflage.
It matters too much how he sees me. I've
never shopped so obsessively. Even having him
on the outskirt of my life is more than I can
afford. In some cultures even today
women hold on to their virginity, for value,
for trade as if without that purity, they're worth-
less. My poems are like my hymen, a little
barrier he wants to plunge thru. Too many
women are in love with him but I have, like a
prized virgin, the mirror few others have to give,
Once he said, seeing a nasty mark on Face Book
he was wounded. Really. we're not so different:
caring too much about what people think.
With me, worried can I dance, can I follow?
He writes so much better than he knows
but wishes he'd finished college or painted.
But on the dance floor to me he's more
than any PhD or National Book Award
winner or Pulitzer Prize. But like anyone in the
fifties who'd say why would we buy a cow when
they can get the milk free, I keep the dance
poems close, let that be an amor, let that be
a lure he'll long for

THE POEMS
LIKE A FLASH OF SKIN

gets him going,
it's as if suddenly
he feels he could
be deep in
that space. Some
thing made him want
this and want it
now. Maybe a lover
left him. Maybe who
wouldn't, he wished
did. Suddenly a
ballroom poem
seemed glistening
and pink to him
excited to have him
enter as he was to
move in for the kill.
Suddenly my words
were the labia he
hadn't stop dreaming
of. Suddenly he knows
what it is to want
what he doesn't
have when so much
he's wanted was
just there, gift
wrapped for him

waiting to be asked to
dance. I didn't know
until that hideous night
no boy would want to
hold me. So I painted,
did science projects
that always won.
First prize with a
study of the eye. It
seemed one way to
have people look at
me. Later, no longer
plump, men yelled
from car windows in
Honolulu and Muscle
Beach. Waiting for
some stud to come
up to me still makes
me sweat. So when my
teacher is hypnotized
by my poems, uses
words like genius

reading my poems to
everyone in the dance
studio, spends so much
time checking my
website out his wife
was miffed. When he
wants to see every
or any poem I've
written about ballroom
and yet doesn't ask
me to demonstrate
like I'm someone he's
never talked to, yet
begs, like someone
settling in to do a blow
job, for poems I've
done about being
at Fred Astaire who
knows how hard he
will have to work to
peel them out of
my cold dead hands

WHY IT'S SOMETIMES
BETTER TO DANCE
WITH A BROOM
THAN A MAN

it won't step on your
feet. Since some men
can't lead, a broom at
least will let you move
over the floor, won't
grab your hand so hard
there's blood in your
palm. A broom keeps
its mouth shut, won't
go on about poodles
and puddles, have bad
breath, wear scratchy
wool. You won't have
bloody toes, bruised
shins or blood stains
on blue suede if it
kicks you and it won't
tell you what it has
no clue about

A YEAR AGO
PRINCE CHARMING SAID
IT PLEASED HIM

he was charmed watching
me and two other better
than I am dancers looking
bored and amused at a small
step the three of us did at
a more advanced level. I
loved, he said, seeing you
so relaxed, having fun. Over
400 days ago and I'm in a
similar class. The other two
dancers have given up dancing
with those men who have
never danced before. Oh sure
there are men on a scale lets
say they go from A for great
to the end of the alphabet
only there aren't enough
letters to tell you how I feel.
Z isn't low enough. No sane
woman would dance with
these men. Wolves would
definitely dance better.
Or horses or cows. And I
got up on a rainy Saturday
for this? I could have stayed
under the heavy blue quilt
with the cat, gone to a ballet
class in another city, typed
up some of the poems written
maybe in a similar fury,
too dazed like now to be
sure what they meant

wasn't the word c-t, cunt
tease? in another era?
How could I not be
up against a player. But
this piece he wants isn't
a little skin. He's
surrounded by that,
he's drowning in Asian
beauties, not a woman
there doesn't come
for his touch. Maybe a few
see thru him but I've
been blinded, dazed.
Just to think it was his
mahogany eyes or how
his hips pressed, made
me go where I should.
How he holds hands
walking to and from the
dance floor. Then I

got it. His voice, maple
syrup with clots of
honey: that's how he
operates. Be furious and
the sugar smooth shuts
you down. There's
nothing I can do. Call
it cunt tease but he
wants something deeper
within, he wants what
only I can give him.
No body parts, no rouge
pink slice of skin. He
doesn't want lips or
nipples. He's all horned
up to get his hands on
poems. He's called them
genius. He's wild to see
how much of himself
he'll see in them

IT ISN'T JUST
DANCING WITH DOLTS

that's sent me into
this rancid mood,
not only that it's a
step I know, could
teach someone else
in 3 minutes. Then
with a few minutes
left in the class, a
miracle, a mirage, a
man who could talk
and smile and move
one foot ahead of
the other, quite
unique this gloomy
day where if I get
thru these 40 minutes
without losing a
finger, a toe or
having my wrist
snapped and my face
filled with bad breath
and the ice of the
teacher I've made my
self believe what
he's not, this life saver
guard at the door
when I feel I'm
drowning, just his
smile, a rope,
reprieve, enough

I WANTED TO WRITE
A POEM ABOUT
THE TANGO'S FLAME

something about the waltz's
silver beauty. I want the
beauty of peacock shimmer
in new light. It's harder
for me to celebrate. Some
how I'm strongest when I'm
bitchy but I wanted a poem
about the high of dancing
with an amazing leader,
of being swept out of the
day and maybe tomorrow,
of moving as startlingly, as
gorgeously as the clothes I
go overboard in, desperate
to look as I'd like to dance.
Someone who doesn't even
write poetry came up with
one praising this dance
teacher's beautiful soul and
tho I'm captive in dreams
as she is, one cold look,
nights he doesn't ask for
what others call obligation
dances with a student and
I go stone. If I was more
bitchy in real life, said what
scalds, this poem might have
gone someplace magical
as someone dancing under
the stars while the rest of
the house is sleeping, stars
on skin, glitter as silver
shadows. But after yesterday
all I feel is sore and bruised

DID I SAY
"WITH A VENGEANCE"
OR "VEHEMENTLY"
WHEN HE ASKED
ABOUT
THE DANCE POEMS

promise I'd write with
vengeance, that would
have been something you
have a feeling about.
Some premonition. I
did want to write some
thing magical as a prom
dress, something that
glitters. It's not my style
but if someone who does
not write can write some
thing exquisite and silver
about him, why can't
I write a dance poem,
sensuous and sweet as
skin moving under thin
green silk or a bride
under lace, luscious
the rhythm of a
belly dancer's body.

IN THE POEM
I WANTED TO WRITE

we moved like birds on
fire, joy was the champagne
we sipped. I wore rose,
stripped of all memory of
the times I never got them.
Each turn was oxygen.
We clicked like glasses of
Beaujolais. The lights
dazzling stars on the floor
as we were in the poem
I couldn't write

THERE WAS A GIRL

don't jump to conclusions.
Yes she was in clothes
that looked like mine
at the edge of the fire
place when suddenly, in
the coals, a man seemed
to leap out. He was a
dancer, a conjuror,
disappearing behind
wild flame only to stand
before her like an oak.
I think of that Indian film
where a woman no man
is wild for marries a
tree. Then his branches
sweep her off, yes,
the old cliché, her feet,
grazed the dance floor.
Then, a sudden leap as if
the spring of a watch
had broken before her.
Velvety, he kept saying
her voice was. It was
the velvety flute sound
that made her remember
this but the waltz shifted
like a building collapsing.
It was all staccato, it
was a dangerous tango.
It was long ago but
the feel of his body
won't dissolve

WHEN I WENT IN
IN A RAGE

when I wore leather
to be tough
just his voice and
I melted. The blood
sun turned the dance floor rose

When I wore leather to be tough
—I just wrote touch but I
meant tough. Later he was touching
my body all over. It's just
part of the class

I just wrote "touch."
Absurd to keep wanting.
Stroking my velvet jacket he
said I should do voice- overs

Absurd to keep wanting more.
Better to keep my poems about him
on hold, even the one that links
him to Obama.

Better to keep my poems about
him as allure. Flirt, just
laugh, get silly about the stick
to keep our frame.
How straight it is, how slippery

Better to be silly and flirt.
Better knowing it's my poems he
holds closest, holds like skin,
imagine when he touches my thighs
and belly its no different from
my cat

Better knowing it's the poems he
lusts for and not think about rage.
So what if he makes those 60
minutes magical

Don't you think that touching is
better than tough? Don't you
think being touched is
better than being tough?

WHEN HE MOLDS

my thigh, more
intimate than many
lovers. When he
uses a stick to
keep the frame
strong and every
thing begins to
have a double
meaning, slippery
(as he is) strong.
"stay erect, no
slumping, be open."
"Think of the woman,"
he grins, let her do
her thing first.
Don't go racing
ahead, forgetting
her

I COULD HAVE
USED HIM
FOR A DART BOARD

I could have bought a
voodoo doll but there
wouldn't be enough
pins to jab him. I
didn't want to pretend
I'd been hating him
for 72 hours. I wore
leather, as if I could
protect what hurt
inside. He said my
voice was velvety.
I was that snaky part
of him that sheds
what it can't still use.
I was camouflaged
as a copperhead. When
he asked me about
my ballroom poems,
he was intrigued,
he was nervous. *Should
I be nervous, should
I be afraid?* he asked,
like a child. Yes, be very
then I ran, shedding
more than I planned to

SOME DAYS,
AS STARTLING

as if Nijinsky
slivered in a side
door, lit up
the mirrors

something from
another world.
When he turned
like an electric dreidel

not a man or a
woman wouldn't
have thrown him

flowers. Diamonds
burned around him,
a circle of candles

Somewhere deeper,
he is growing in
a hot house

if he stays,
you'll live like
a leaf and die
like a rose

WHY THE POEMS
ABOUT THE ONES
I WANTED THE MOST
DON'T TURN OUT
AS NICE POEMS

because my obsession with
dark eyed mahogany hair
that turned logic to mush.

because my obsession with dark eyes
was too strong a magnet

There is always something
exotic: the Fatimis, Agasipours, ok there
was a black haired lake blue eyes
Murphy. But so few blondes,

so few who weren't damaged: a torn
heart, Iraq blasted off leg. The one

who couldn't hear, still
wanting to hear from me
and now the one, totally inaccessible
to me, a baby, a mystery

whose dance moves hypnotize now
asks *What about the ballroom*

dance poems. When are you bringing
me some. He won't want to see them

FOR THE MEN
WHO CAN'T LEAD

soggy, flaccid as a
penis that can't do
what it should
either. Little limp
hands, not that
I want my rings
crushed into skin
in what surrounds
them like a neglected
dog collar imbedded
in fur. Please, no
smelly men and
please no wool. And
don't think yanking
my arm out of its
socket is a lead then
bitch that I'm not
following. Give
me a man who
knows where we are
going, who's got
his eyes on the prize,
knows his destination
and goes for it. I
want a man who will
put his legs deep
between mine when
we tango, not a vise
but a setting
holding a jewel

BALLROOM

I don't want men
who reek of garlic.
I've learned I can
keep from gagging
if it isn't too strong
but the stink of
bad breath and
dirty clothes gets
to me. And wool,
ok I'm strange,
even cashmere
gives me a rash.
Don't kick me so
hard there's blood
on the polished
floor or squeeze
my hand so hard
my ring leaves a
permanent bruise.
If I have to dance
with you ok but
please no more
stories about it
raining poodles and
if this is your
first class, don't
tell me your version
of the correct Fox
Trot frame. Or
tell me I'm wrong.
And if you've got a
hard on and think
it will make me want
to want you, think
a minute. If you
sweat so, don't
imagine those drop-
lets are perfuming
the air like star
flowers or sweet
notes of music

FOR THE MEN
WHO CAN'T LEAD

don't race ahead
like a runaway train,
oblivious, unsure
I'm still with you.
Don't jerk me in one
direction then the
next, yanking my
arm out of its socket.
I'm not 6 four and
if you are, be careful.
No wonder some
times the woman
leans her head back
to the left, except in
promenade when
there's no chance of
having to smell the
other's breath. They
do have mints in a
jar. Please use them.
Don't grab for a
woman's boobs or
crotch or whistle or
snap your fingers.
And don't snarl, get
snarky with your
girlfriend or wife
so every step is like
pushing pianos
and you make #234,
top of the ball
room jerk list

IF WE COULD
JUST CLONE
A FEW DECENT
MEN BLUES

don't need
marines
or studs,
don't need
actors or princes.

Just a few who can
lead a tango, a bolero.
They don't have to

look like male models
tho that shouldn't
stand in the way. Just

a few would help so
when I move
from one who knocks

his partner to the
floor, relief will be
waiting, two minutes

with just one who
can dance. I'm not
asking for much

THERE ARE
BALLROOM DANCERS OF FIRE

nothing like snowflakes
but like an unending spark.
I bet even asleep they are
burning with expectation.
One man flies across the
dance floor, a blaze when
he walks in the room.
He's not even Russian.
Something in his blood boils
like a ballet dancer who,
asked if she wants to live,
says "I want to dance."

THE LAST DANCE

petals fall from
the vase of orchids.
The girls pale as
the flowers, sitting
thru what should
be the most special
waltz, their pastel
smiles. He looks
away from the
other beauties.
In the arms of the
one she won't stop
imagining will be
hers, what you
can't see, she is
falling like the petals,
naked in fawn and
rose lace

IN THE DREAM

Dark doors glitter,
light as a ballerina
with feet of rose
petals. On my wrists,
jasmine and the
scent of sex French
women I've heard
dab behind their ears.
Nothing but rubies
and tuber rose in
my hair, I melt into
others. This chain
of light, this moving
thru phosphorescence
and then, holding the
one I never could,
moving together
like young trees with
wind on their branches

LATER SHE'D REMEMBER

dancing along the Charles
with the man she couldn't marry.
Fireflies, like miniature flashlights.
In photographs the Sycamore
breeze twists their hair together.
"To my angel" and love on
the back. Moving like birds on
fire they danced past benches of
lovers. It was the last dance
before she eloped. Words were
turned to weapons. When she was,
she was more there than ever,
would always be beautiful with
only pearls and jasmine in her hair

SOMETIMES BALLROOM IS LIKE
SUICIDE ON THE METRO TRACKS

you just turn your head and wail. Only
you're not the conductor but really
it's the same. You are about to jump
toward arms that move right past you.
It happens a dozen times. One driver said
after the first time you just turn your
head and wait for impact. That is me
in a special glitzy shimmery mini but
the best dancer doesn't stop. The impact of
course is in my head. Sometimes I'd imagine
he looks in the rear view mirrors, can see me
tumbling in the air just flying as I care more
than I ought to about not flying thru the
dance floor. He'll never go over that image,
won't feel it's happening in front of him right
now, but as a chubby girl not asked to dance at
high school sock dance, I see it happening
over and over. I'm the one with a mental snap
shot of horror as he barrels down and moves
right past me, a sense of overwhelming helplessness
and anger. Those after shocks won't let me sleep,
the intensity of rejection wilder than intimacy,
the trauma being entangled with his ice. I could
make up excuses like relatives of jumpers do: he lost
his mind at the last minute. Or does he see me as
as dangerous, a jumper into violence? Is he really scared
I might write something dark about him? Too many
nights are the same. It doesn't matter at what speed
you're going, I'm flattened, a mess and yet I know I'll
get right back on like the train operators with their
wide wind shields with wide screen clarity or a woman
timing her jump, as the train enters, hits the window,
a bird, spread eagled

WHEN I READ ABOUT
A MILLION-YEAR-OLD PRIMATE

bridging the evolutionary gap.
It was a jolt : I've been dancing
with this primate, in drag, of
course, as a man, the last weeks
of ballroom. Long arms, short
legs. I recognize that starving
look and there were flecks of
bark in his cuffs, probably
from eating the trees. He
grabbed my arm like he was
swinging from branch to
branch. He had a smell and I
swear he had food in his arms.
Or maybe he thought I was
food. Maybe that was it. He
seemed suited for the trees. I know
they are studying bones and
silt and sand but take it from me:
he lived and he still does. I
don't know what he'll evolve
into. Now I know why he talked,
at least you could call it that,
about figs and palms—they grow
where he did, where it was wet
and teaming with birds. He still
uses his finger bones as if digging
into my skin. I told him it hurt.
He's got a brain but tho he walks
upright, he's not much of a
dancer. Some think he is a
treasure trove of surprises. I'd
be happy, just come to the dance
studio and I'll send him back

THE MAD GIRL
IS STILL HAUNTED
BY GHOSTS OF THE NIGHT
OF THE SOCK DANCE

it's as much part of
her as a blue concentration
camp tattoo. It defines
her. It is blue that does
not dissolve, spreads
deeper thru her body.
You don't see it under
her Betsey Johnson and
Bebe clothes. She imagines
she can disguise it,
camouflage how she shakes.
When any man who matters
moves close then passes her
by to dance with another
she feels sick. She could
pay scads of face time with
a pro, like buying a gigolo,
admitting that's the only
way she'll get what she
wants

THE MAD GIRL
IS AFRAID
OF BEING ASKED
TO DANCE,
AFRAID OF NOT
BEING ASKED TO
DANCE

lately, even when one
man comes close or if
she's paired up in soul
trail, she's becoming
terrified as a woman
who hasn't dated for
years, wants to but is
frightened that her
body isn't the same
body she had before
when the boys touched
her breasts, isn't
sure whether to help
him unhook or sprint
out the door

THE MAD GIRL IS STILL
THE CHUBBY GIRL
ON THE BLEACHERS
WAITING ALL NIGHT
AND NO ONE ASKS HER
TO DANCE

A friend told her yesterday
"it's odd, what men didn't
like in high school they go
for now: they like brains
and that you've written or
painted something, are a
lawyer, a surgeon." But
the mad girl isn't sure
it's any better. Sure, she's
had lovers galore but she
just wants to dance with
someone special. He's in
love with her poems. People
used to think she was them,
offered drugs when she
went to read. The one
who just one dance would
make her high, adores
her poems he says, raves
and quotes lines. He hugs
her at parties. She knows she
shouldn't care but she
feels her face burn as it
did when the boys climbed
the bleachers, her heart
pounding and then sinking
as they walked past

THE MAD GIRL
IS STILL STUCK
AT THE TERRIBLE
HIGH SCHOOL
PROM NIGHT

its more years than
seem possible since
but it might have
been yesterday. Dolled
up, not realizing she
wasn't as wanted,
at least danced with
as the rest. Now she
has her own man, true
but she wants to feel
pulled from the real
world. She wants to
spin and float out of
her fear, out of the
every day with its
dishes and cat food.
She wants the intensity
of what can't last, drug
like, flaming, a bird
on fire falling thru
what blazes and burns
out and dies just for
the length of a waltz

WHEN NO ONE ASKS HER TO DANCE

the mad girl dies a little
inside, she faces like an
old Betsey Johnson dress.
What's always made her
face burn, her sense of a
man coming toward her,
wanting to hold her,
then slithering past to some
one right behind. Her hair
goes lank, gold bracelets
melt. She might have
been wearing Cinderella
pre-ball raggedy char
maid clothes. This does
not happen, just one time.
When she goes home,
only the Internet waits
for her, beckons, a silver
skirt, sequins from Betsey
Johnson. They promise
to hold her close as
her skin, to dazzle any
one who comes near.

After a night waiting on
the sidelines, wanting to
be the one men don't
move past, she knows
she'd come nude if she
had her old body. Instead,
she's made a moat of
silk, black sequins and
lace (almost funereal),
see thru tunics, jeans so
tight, one more pound
and they'd split. Each
month Visa comes she
vows this is the last time
but then when she feels
invisible to all the blue
eyed men she dials 1-800,
goes to Bebe or Free People,
maybe Nordstrom's wild
for something that will
stop one of them in his
tracks like the red lights
of an ambulance

THE MAD GIRL
DOESN'T KNOW
WHAT TO DO
WITH ALL THE CLOTHES

It's not that she didn't
have too many, gave 60 bags
to Salvation Army, clothes
never worn. Little jerseys and
sweats. Forget the pile
in her closet of jeans, the
box of leather pants but in
ballroom the world is
different. Ok, it wasn't
always this bad but once she's
obsessed, nothing can save
her. If she can't be the
best dancer, she'll let her
clothes be a mask, hide how
it hurts when her dance
teacher dances with every
other woman, leaves her sure
she'll screw up anything
when she dances near him. So,
instead of valium or prozac
or booze, she goes to clothes
on the internet: six black minis:
satin, tulle, velvet, lace.
Who knows what will be
most eye catching. It doesn't
matter she's thin as a model, triple
small, triple zero. After being
pudgy in high school, sure
pretty clothes were for someone
else, stress and tragedy worked
better than dieting and pills.
If someone says they only see

her in dresses, she orders a
dozen new stretch skinny jeans.
The clothes, more and more
a mask: sequins that dazzle and
distract you from seeing the
blues, that black and blue
inside her eating all light tho
she sparkles and smiles,
at least tries to

BOXES PILE IN THE MAD GIRLS ROOM

rooms she wants spare
as she is, under 100 lbs.
Nothing she can't use
on her body but you
can't see pounds of
longing that despite
how she tries to starve
herself, balloon. So she
orders a skirt from
Bebe—make it sixteen
skirts. She wears them
to attract what she's sure
otherwise can't. Of
course the high lasts as
long as some men's attention
to any woman does:
under 40 minutes so she
goes on to the next,
a little glitz, a little silk,

skirts of lace. The clothes
are piled on tables,
some good enough
to keep, some go back
immediately. She tries
them on for hours like
models in a department
store, something she was
asked to do when time
didn't seem so important.
Now, boxes pile on
boxes in the dining room, in
the garage. When they
came, they seemed
like gifts, as one's charm
did, his wild attention. Now
they seem like clutter
and debris and too high
a price, much too expensive

SOMETIMES, OR
AT LEAST BEFORE
WHEN I'M NOT
WONDERING
WHAT NEXT

just seeing him on the floor
dancing with a pro or newbie
made me pleased. That
was before it was a relief
to have him out of the
country or thinking of
going to China myself.
Sometimes, just his look,
the tilt of his bones. Not
the most handsome, not the
world's best dancer but
was it something, eyes,
maybe that voice I know I
fell for before anything.
Now I think it was how he
moved in a direction: You
could see he knew where he
was going and nothing
could stop him. (Once
he whacked into me, I was
stunned but because it was
him, it was thrilling) I
should have taken this as a
warning but I was dazed,
hypnotized

AFTER THE CLASS

the glow of his
"your voice, you
should talk over
films." Then we
have the dance
pole: *keep it straight.*
hold it right, of
course it's slippery,
just get it where
it should be.
The hugs, the kiss,
the *you are a*
genius: you've got
the dance, it's your
partner. And then,
like a gooey gigolo
until it's time for
the next private lesson,
I'm invisible to him.
I'm not there

THE POEM
I WANTED TO WRITE

is the one where I can
just admire how he
holds a woman on
stage, how he knows
where he's moving
and I see the beauty
in the shapes he makes
on the floor. If I hear
his voice, it's a plus
like seeing wild
eagles from the porch

IN THE POEM
I WANTED TO WRITE

I would be invisible
as fireflies under snow.
I would watch his
grace, hear his voice
from a distance,
objective, impassive
as cats that see things
as they are. They
wouldn't confuse a
kiss, a few words for
plates of sardines
or the warm cove of
arms as some
permanent address.
In the poem I want to
write, I would be
graceful as cats, and
beautiful. I could be
stretching out in
the beauty of his
moves as they do
patches of sun and
know it moves on,
how light will appear
in other places

I WANT TO WRITE A POEM

to frame that, what is
it? More than charm?
Some love of women
that is as much a part
of him as breathing.
He can't help it and
the women can't too.
Simple as a cat
hypnotized by light
reflected from rhine
stones spattered
across the room. No
one loves the wildness
of sequins and diamonds
more than I do. I want
to write a poem that
isn't a dark poem
where I want to die
when he walks across
the floor to ask another
woman. Be a cat, I
tell myself, calm as
monks meditating,
trapped on a raft
knowing if rescue comes,
it comes and if it's
snow and blackness,
it's snow and
blackness

THE POEM
I WANT TO WRITE

would be like
just watching him.
Let's say it's Broad-
way. He says he feels
he's on Broadway
every day. But this
time it *would* be
Broadway. Why
not? He's in the spot
light, as if he wasn't
always. I'd be safe,
shadowed. No wonder-
ing if he'll ask me
to dance. Be invisible
as he moves past
me to another woman.
I can stare, luxuriate in
whatever it is that
hypnotizes. I don't
have to care if he'll
feel my stare or vanish
around the corner

THE POEM I WANT TO WRITE

unless you've ESP
you won't find me.
I'll vanish like the
first image I used
in my first poem,
snow flakes in a
burning palm. I
need to not be in
the poem, another
one of your groupies,
wild for a few minutes
in your arms. The
poem should be
you sipping sake
in a café warm
enough to eat out
side tho there is
snow still in the
mountains. Your
wife and son the
only light you need.
The last light would
slide down into
twilight. It would be
enough that it
gets dark early, the
leaves let go
as I have

I CARRY TOO MUCH
OF YOU WITH ME

not my intent. I'd
prefer to travel alone.
Your light blinds.
I don't want your
world colliding
wildly. Too much
of it careens into my
space. Where did you
learn to "drive?"
So elegant: tango
and foxtrot—still the
time you crashed
into me in the waltz.
It started with that
concussion I think.
Bits of you like a
burning star rocketing
and leaving me changed,
a secret I kept from
myself like the
woman from Law
and Order raped at knife
point on the crowded
subway. Was she
thrilled? Was she
so terrified she had
no idea how it
came to that?

THE POEM
I WANTED TO WRITE

wouldn't be the one I
couldn't show you
but something I might
write about a dead
lover, not just the rage
I'm free to say but all
that's too adoring. You
never will take with
you what no one else
knows, like leaving
a poem with half the lies
left out. In the poem I
can't write there are
ordinary moments with
you. Heartache has
no where to hide.
I will never dance from
sheets like a wife.
I will never dance as
I want to with you

LIKE BALLROOM

he does his steps and to
hell with me. The instructor
says you're doing the same
step but you are not doing
them with her. You go
like she isn't there. For
the male dancer think *pas de
deux*—think how the male
ballet dancer is like a
frame for the woman. He
shows her off and protects
her. She is the one we
want to see. Delicate,
beautiful, supported. She
needs you but men should
not have to know that.
Out from the dance floor,
the advice evaporates.
"I'm not Prince Albert"
he says, "you don't have
to walk behind me," and
back on the floor, he
refuses to pause, let me
finish one step to go on to
the next. We are doing the
same steps but not at
the same time, not in
not in synch. It's not in
the same direction

TOO EARLY SUNDAY
ON THE METRO

I'd have stayed in a
cocoon of darkness.
Instead, since it's
not rainy or ice and
no one I know is
dying, I head to
Silver Spring as if
an hour at the barre
could snap me out of
grief, deaden the
blackness in me the
way others head for
the bar. It's before 9
AM. Some carry
shopping bags, or
head to Union station.
Grocery carts for
early birds. It's cool
enough for a parka
tho by noon it could
be sweltering or rain.
One woman's dolled
up in spikes and
heavy jasmine perfume
maybe on the way
to meet her lover
whose wife is at church.
The leaves hardly
changing from
yesterday but on the way
to letting go too

SOMETIMES IN TANGO

the closeness stuns,
close as they say
two photons fired thru
a slit stay paired
to the end of time.
There are dancers—
do you think it's me,
polarized to change
its spin while the other
(don't make me say)
a not you do a u turn
on a dime, fly apart
at speeds of light and
never touch again.
Sometimes for no
reason on the metro
it seems you are close
as in a tango. Sometimes
your scent, the way
your mouth moves
comes flying back. Who
knows what violence
fuses particles, what
keeps what's paired
paired. I don't need
much, just to be
entangled as when
in tango only your hips,
the music moves me
and I know this is the way

THE MAD GIRL WANTS
TO SING "GOT ALONG
WITHOUT YOU
BEFORE I MET YOU"

she knows she'll get along.
Some of her paintings show that.
First he is in the frame with
her, then, he's not. The back
ground colors change from
a sea blue and sun bright
to muted greys, color of black
swans and midnight skies
no moon lives in. Then her
canvas is more like the darkest
Rothko paintings, a square
no figures, no shapes stain.
He, who knows everything
about dance frames has
walked out of hers

THE MAD GIRL NEVER
ISN'T HUNTING
FOR SOMETHING

a contact lens, a contact.
With all her black velvet,
it isn't odd she can't find
black velvet top #74
in a closet of midnight
licorice shimmer, not
absurd she forgets the
dance tops buried in the
crammed closet. There
is no light and even if
there was, it's unlikely
she'd find them. Danskin
tops, stacked so deep,
one move and the tower
would crumble. The mad
girl, needing more she
is sure than any others,
has more paper, more
rings, more lovers, more
photographs, more grief,
more insomnia, more
lipstick, more Betsey
Johnson and Bebe, more
anger, more bruises.
But it's paper and clothes
that have made a moat
around her, a mountain
of books, an avalanche
about to sweep her
up as she hunts a note
book, a camisole, a
poem that she is sure,
without, she can't go on

THE MAD GIRL FEELS BALLROOM
HAS BECOME POISONOUS

forget she used to feel
all there was left was
to swirl in his arms.
Forget he still cares
about, quotes a line
from her poem, the
next day he's ice and
she's frozen, feels
burned by his cold,
can't follow him
even on the dance
floor. "Follow me
bitch," from another
direction, enough,
"one more word and
I'm leaving, going
home." It's military,
it's Nazi Germany,
the kiss of death march

tango, the Russian
roulette rumba. She
never knows how
deadly the night will
be. If she had what
ever pills Michael
Jackson swallowed,
if she saw any other
way out. If something,
a word, a look that
wasn't a weapon
could soothe her. If too
often she sensed that
there isn't much time
was the most comforting
thing, maybe she could
end the poem and
who knows what else
in a less dark dark way

THE MAD GIRL
HEARS A LULLABY
AT THE BARRE

no not a bar bar
but the ballet barre.
It's the morning after
a nightmare night
and tho things could
be worse and probably
will be, she's shattered,
feels blighted, feels
unconnected to any
body still in the
world. She feels like
a blackened toe
about to flake off.
The toe it hardly seems,
like so much of her,
ever was part of
her and then
the pianist plays
what sounds like a
lullaby and if it's not
it might as well have
been. Nothing has soothed
and held her this way,
nothing has made
her feel lulled
and held in softness
she almost feels
she could
float in

ON ONE OF THOSE
BREAK YOUR HEART
CAJUN FIDDLE NIGHTS

before shutters bang
and the moon's camouflaged

Somewhere else, a woman
out to pick up a video

veers off the road
while her husband lathers

shampoo on their auburn-
haired daughter,

her pajamas just out of
the dryer, laughing

as bubbles spill into the
air. I walk thru wet

grass, the fireflies
lie down finally. The

musky night heat
is a drug where I touch and

drift thru starlight
toward morning

as that woman, in the wet
grass, not still waiting

never will

WHEN THERE AREN'T
ENOUGH WORDS
FOR THE BLUES

tourmaline, sapphire, azure,
robin's egg, sky or baby,
blue bonnet blue, iris, lake
or sea or even teal blue,
turquoise. When they
over flow, bury mid
August in their dark navy,
then midnight. When
there aren't enough
words for blue, the paint
chip blues, 70 of them,
wouldn't be blue
enough. This month
of too many dark
anniversaries, the blue
chicory taking over
abandoned lots,
feeling as abandoned,
bruise blue, blues all
around, the light
leaving two minutes
earlier each day,
leaving the
why-didn't-we blues,
summer running down.
Where are you?

YOU CAME, AS SO OFTEN,
UP FROM THE VALLEY

sure I've been waiting,
wanting you, waiting
and then you, under
my hair. Not you with
your Cuban motion,
fingers that hold any
woman's hand walking
from the dance floor.
Not the you, you but
the idea of your mouth,
skin braided with
longing. I've been
swamped by sea blues,
star gaze and billow
blue. It's not enough.
And what to do with
my skin smelling of
your hair's darkness,
obvious as prostitutes
in Kabul tapping
their feet under them

AUGUST 27

flat, all the way
to Canada. 65 and the
hideous tropic rain
gone. Some
thing over. A back
to school fall sky.
I'm sleeping in the
car to escape as if
there'd be nights with
a finger nail moon
and you again, with
that grin, my black
dress on the floor

THE DREAM OF TERRY

suddenly there on the train
to Oslo. And me, there,
figuring it's ok, imagining
what, an affair? A hook
up? Is it too late for that?
So he was a student of mine
in another life, not one
who made my face burn,
made me shiver like Sal
Falova but a skinny good old
boy who loved poetry so
much he salted away one of
the only two copies of
one of my books in
his military trench coat. Those
days with writing work shops
at my house, at St Rose
where I read poems too
scandalous for some
but the nuns adored them.
Summer of divorce
and Terry was there, often, as
if ready to step in tho it was
not for me. I got my book
back, never gave him what he
wanted. Sometimes a poem
of his in a magazine. Same
formal, almost academic
piece about a Kentucky field
or the last thoughts of a
Confederate general. So many
years in other cities, never a
thought of his stillness,

forgetting maybe he took me
home after I drank too
much to get thru a reading—
old enough to have a son the
age he was. Just a few words
at a reading back in town,
no electricity, 5 minutes talk
maybe and then I slid back
to Virginia. So how am
I hip to hip, my head on his
shoulder heading past
snow peaks? Oslo, already
with its warming quilts,
mugs of mulled wine and
this feeling a feeling, a
freshness I haven't felt
for too long

DREAM OF SNAKES

I've left ballet or maybe
ballroom, am walking
or on a street— is it
49th? near the bus station
in NYC. I hate walking
there, am hurrying,
avoiding eyes. 9 blocks
farther I realize I don't
have my shoes. I've been
walking in worn socks.
I'm only part way home.
If it starts to rain and
there's glass in the road.
I shudder but going back
to find the clogs seems
horrendous. This is not
the way I expected things,
imagining a break, that
I could curl up in a
quilt with hot chocolate
and my sweet Aby, Jete
not this panic and certainly
not, as I finally round the curve
home, two snakes, huge
and thick as a poplar tree,
maybe a maple. I try to
play it cool until I see
one edging along the crowd
toward me, head at a tilt,
rearing up

6TH DAY BACK

the hugs and the
small waves stop

I stash my heart
in my spike ballroom

shoes. I've
word knives waiting.

Got a headache,
some bad news.

Nothing short of
death is an excuse

for this coldness.
Nothing is acceptable

That you fill every
room you're not

in is sickening. Just
want me and I

can let you go

Horses

THE MAD GIRL
STRADDLES TWO LIVES
LIKE HORSES
GOING IN DIFFERENT
DIRECTIONS

something inside her
feels about to split
like those prisoners
pulled by stallions,
one east, one west.
She breathes fantasy,
in the mint of his
lips and his hips
against her. Once a
week this fire leaves
a stain, tattoo that
tells its own story.
She goes through the
other life, feeds the
cat, stamps the mail.
You wouldn't recognize
her in Betsey Johnson
tulle and velvet, tuber
rose scented skin
for the mirage. Unreal
except for how her
ballroom shoes
wear thinner, the
sole a membrane
shriveling like a
hymen as she puts on
sweats and sneakers,
fleece for the space
between what is
and could be

HORSES AT MIDNIGHT,
NOT A SLIVER OF MOON

maples, rain soaked
would blur car lights
if there were any

somewhere, the
sound of a train.
Then I was a long-

legged beauty. Then
my hair was fire.
The rain erased

the space between
our bodies. Later
you write I was

stunning. Too late,
too long after I
didn't imagine that

ON A WEDNESDAY
I REFUSE TO WRITE
ABOUT YOU

you are like sleep, impossible
to have if I'm desperate.
Instead, I'll dwell on the
showers of meteors, on
the ponds lilac and mauve
ripples as light goes away
earlier. August crickets
get louder. Somewhere
else, a woman who sees
ghost horses talks to her
dead mare. She sees the
dead jockeys gulp after
a morning breeze. The
coffee she smells in their
gloved hands, much more
real than too much I
have swallowed.

THE WOMAN
WHO SEES
DEAD HORSES

there, suddenly, she
says there, on the
race track: ghost
horses. Jockeys
and trainers. Rail
birds, yes, but it
was the horses.
They would exercise
themselves in the
mornings, even
run in races with
live horses. Maybe
why some of the
horses racing spook.
It seems there are
no reasons. The
dead horses are not
able to rest. They
are dangerous
to live horse and
jockeys, these ghost
horses that haven't
gone into the
light haunt race
tracks across the
country. She said she
did all she could,
sometimes she had
to ask the ghost
jockeys and grooms
to lead one fiery
stallion too wild to
do anything with. She
thinks he is still
probably there

she was looking down
when someone took
their photo holding
the reins of a pony. \
She stares off to the
side watching some
thing out of the range
of the lens. She is not
smiling. Her socks
crumple. She clutches
the horse reins as if
already dreaming
of escape. She's
already turning away
from this house, her
room the smallest
in the house. Maybe
sick nights in the den,
her father sure she was
asleep whispering to

the hired girl,
whispering pussy,
pussy, nice pussy.
So many nights like
a mirror she stood
watching her self in
wondering who she
was and how she came
to be there, imagining
these days will melt
like clay her mother
will years later
help her daughter
to shape. She sits in
her small room,
stares at peonies in
the moon, something
inside her already
grabbing those reins

LATE JULY
SUMMER NIGHT
NEARLY

gray fox slither
past, stunning as
the dancer whose
body hypnotizes.
Something in
the trees, loud
as wood ducks.
A deer steals
past apple boughs.
A saved mare
nuzzles her grain
bucket as if it
were her foal, as
if she somehow
knows how close
her long dark was

LATE JULY

night birds
with their legs
locked on twigs
deep in branches.

Orion's belt,
a swirl of rhine
stone. Lily
petals clenched

like a woman
composing her
self like a
licorice mare

in the jade
pasture, unsure

what is about
to unfold

HOLIDAY METRO BLUES

leaving in the rain.
Is it a dark front
moving in or
maybe it's the
kiss of all that's
gone, gone love,
gone horses,
mother. The
train rocks, a
Wednesday night
in the no moon
dark wet, a
Wednesday dark
wet, a blues
lullaby, a jab
to remind
me there is so
much left
to lose

POEM WITH A LINE
I CAN'T RESIST
BORROWING
NOT THE ONLY THING
I CAN'T RESIST

when what's most real is
what I can't have in dreams.
When I forget to lock
the door, drunk on his
words, his mouth, his
"I've never known any
one who is so many
different people." When
its lilac raining like
it is tonight and I know
you're more with
me on this paper.
Horses run along the
shore. "And you know
I am good," you write,
what I still am not
sure I never will

YES HE'S GLAD
TO SEE MORE SKIN

when black velvet slips.
Magnolia raining like
it is late after noon.
Someone else gives
me words like a hand
on my shoulder. He
thinks what I touched
was your skin, that
you were inside as
of course you are.
Then he's relieved,
writes, "you were
probably where you
needed to be. Poems
really happen, yours
do. That is real enough."
He writes if he had
the reality of his own
poems, he'd have
fewer scars. As for
you, the one haunting
me, if I never ride a
horse thru your ebony
hair, sleep inside your
brain like that magnolia
rain, I'll still have my
own scars from this
most dangerous tango

WITH YOU

dangerous and seductive

the way you fall in love
with a horse
when you shouldn't

imagine, are fearless

What pulls you in,
beautiful as the

name Raspberry Mist.
Then, the filly's run into

in Kentucky blue grass,
hit so hard she died

of shock. But her
head was up and she was

going to get up. She
still thought

there was more
as I did

to do

Madlove

I'M STUNG, YOUR EYES

it's not only how huge
they are, their darkness

they nudge longing, a
bird under my hair

crying or calling. It
doesn't stop

this bird is my
bird, the bird

of my aloneness.
Wild for more,

never enough
clothes or words
or lips or poems

You might think I
know what I want,

am desperate for it,
can't stop asking

Even when the
ache stops beating

its wings I need
to be wanting

you even now in the
metro it goes on

LIKE A CAT
BRUSHING
AGAINST YOUR CALF

the sense of you,
suddenly rubbing my
skin, almost ESP,
not a ghost, you're
too much alive

suddenly, electricity,
some radio on a timer
under my skin. Sometimes
nothing comes in,
a dead zone

like on the Taconic.
I could go for miles
and there's nothing.
Then, the zap, like
the look of your

eyes across the room.
When there's nothing
I wonder, are you
feeding your baby
getting it on with

your wife and then
like a news bulletin
blotting out the
rest it's there.
Was this what
telegrams did?

Is this a startling
mirage. Were
the margaritas too?

WITH YOU

I could be a drunk.

You could be what
I swore I wouldn't
long for then can't
resist. Just a small
gulp. Doesn't have
to be champagne.
That cold lip,
your lip. I imagine
bending to fit my
mouth over it like
someone kissing a
sleeping child

LIKE A CHILD
RUNNING NAKED
INTO THE SHALLOWS

singing *I'm naked, naked*
as if the pink body under
her arms might slip away.
Trying to sleep, I say your
name over and over. It
doesn't help. Next, warm
milk, a quarter of a valium.
Something like feeling
eyes on you in a crowded
room and you turn around
and the one who matters
is staring at you. I felt some
thing just walking to the
train, feel you. Is it ESP
or more the way after a
cat dies you're caught by
a shape just behind you,
imagine fur against your
leg and of course no
thing is there

WITH YOU IT WAS

like being with the
Hawaiian spirits,
Night Marchers. They
haven't gone, jumped
to the other world
but are stuck in a ghost
like state to wander.
Who knows where you
are during the day but if
there is a full moon,
you're there. With you
I feel like those houses
that ghosts walk right
thru, not that I haven't
left the doors to every
thing I have open. You
still fill dreams. Some
time I'm sure what
chokes me is you.
Choking ghost, other
worldly player. Other
times I feel you are
right there, on the quilt,
in the stained blue sheet.
You "talk storied" me
till I believed it. When I
write your name, I
feel your fingers. In
last night's dream I
couldn't push you away

THE I'M IN A LAWN CHAIR DREAM WITH A IN THE TUB, THE CLOSEST I'VE COME TO HAVING HIM

it's the old, if you stop wanting
something so wildly,
then it happens movie in
darkness. Lets say lately
fantasy is what is and it's
all avatar and this avatar
is flesh, more real than
when he's holding me in
tango, hips rolling toward
where they should. In
the dream, it's summer,
a blue lake. My body's
perfect enough to wear
a string bikini I know will
be in a puddle around
my jeweled toes but it's
this moment, suspended

between what I've ached
for and what, if I could
keep going on and never
come back from, I would.
No scars, my skin as it
was, my hair thicker. Rose
scent on my bare taut legs
and wrist, gashes in my
skin dissolving. I'm a film
in film run backward
until he's about to
step out, unfold me as
he unfolds the towel. I
want to freeze this moment,
stay on the verge of,
waiting for what else
will unfold to unfold

THE POEM
I CAN'T WRITE
ABOUT YOU

isn't the one with you in
the claw foot tub in the
dream. It doesn't have
you in a Karaoke
bar sipping a martini
as mariachi jazzes
Sunday light. Let an-
other write of the joy
in you, your depth.
I see a darkness I
can't braid to me in a
flirt, for a heart beat.
But, then, fantasy these
days is where what isn't
is more real, takes
over what isn't

THE MAD GIRL FEELS
LIKE A PRAYING MANTIS

about to leap, bite
the neck of her prey,
put everything she has
into him. She is wild to
paralyze him, keep
him as her slave.
Don't call her Jezebel
or Medea, don't
look at her with a
sneer. She's been
waiting, his body a
taunt, a lure. It's
nature, it's not fair.
And even if she has
to die soon after,
she will have him
on the sheets
of paper

EASIER MAYBE
IF YOU WERE
A MIRAGE, THAT

phosphorescence, glittering
on the surface of oceans no
one can get to. Sure, I was
wild for, I couldn't escape
until they died. That's a lie:
the hole where they were
and then weren't, only got
louder. And what to make
of the rumor that you and
a blues singer hooked up
in a city where nothing like
that is supposed to get out.
Easier to concentrate on
something I don't like
about you, there must
be something

HER POEM ABOUT YOU

He pulled me out of work,
it was folded into itself
like an about to open up
leaf. Sometimes it's hard
to tell if what you hear
is pain and distress or
joy. Sun off the lake he
said was blinding. The
mariachi band. He was
drinking margaritas. Why
did he show me her love
for him? Was it to say
this can't compare
to what I'd write, or
have? Oh, she didn't say
love but she sure was
subtle. A not so hot but
not terrible poem, how
deep he was. Was
that unconscious? Was
it that she wanted him
deep inside? She could have
taken her wild need and
bought a very pricey
designer dress. But she
wrote the poem. So
in love with. Everyone
felt she would risk
being foolish. And then
to have an artist paint
them both, a sketch.
At least she had
a souvenir

THE MAD GIRL IS UNDONE BY
VELVET SCARVES AND MEN

it's not that she doesn't have many,
has had enough, more than most.
But it's the ones that do her
wrong, misbehave, are torn from
her that haunt. Black velvet
ripped from her neck as she looked
in Hallmarks. Then, last night,
pale, almost a white flesh velvet
one falls from her arms, not unlike
the lover she wants wrapped as
close, would give up dignity,
drunk on him as someone
plastered in a bar who will beg
his, any shoulder to lean on, hold,
sure she's so high on him she
can't walk or think right

WE MUST, HE SAYS,
SCHEDULE A TIME
TO JUST TALK POETRY,
HE SAYS

another day, that
would have been
enough. You'd
think he was any
lover rolling from
the light each
morning deep
into me. Can you
imagine us as
thunder blurs
the panes, doves,
swans under the
deck in the tall
grass? Let me
tell you what isn't,
is louder than that
rain that dissolves
faster than yellow
from the goslings.
You would never
be someone to
hold me, would
look somewhere
else, your eyes
more savage after
a first few years.
As if even those
scattered pearls
were enough to
savor, would be
enough to have
if I had them

WHEN I READ PHILIP ROTH SAID

I cannot and do not live in the world
of discretion, not as a writer anyway.
I would prefer to, I assure you, it would
make life easier. But discretion is,
unfortunately, not for novelists

I think, after that night, is
there a hint of my rose scent?
To be discrete, I could say
perhaps I forgot, mixed
up one novelist for another.
Who knows after those
glasses of scotch. Since I
was the only woman at
the colony and I wasn't quite
twenty, wouldn't he remember
my still perfect skin before
a car slashed into me and
scalped my forehead? 120
stitches. Of course it might
have been someone more
discrete who saw me in a
dusty rose jersey near a bush
the same rouge, dusky as
a nipple, the inside of
lips. I won't vow it was
Philip who invited me to his
cabin for a drink and so
nervous—I'd read all his
books and of course knew
his reputation and thank
God had my own story I
hoped would charm. How
in a weird way we were
connected by my ex-husband's

relatives who sold whole
sale artificial limbs. I
told him stories about what
they had said about him
belching in a TV interview
where to their horror he
drank out of a soda
can. To be discrete, I won't
tell you the place or the
year or why I couldn't let
him inside me but to
be a little less so, I will tell
you he told me the bj I
gave him was especially
heavenly

WITH THAT ONE
NOW, DEAD LOVE

it was the same,
something wild and
rare as Siberian
tigers born in
captivity, nothing
you'd expect.
If the mother
doesn't kill them,
who knows about
the chill cement
floor. Somewhere
else a man straps
explosives to
a belt. There's
not much time.
Too soon to the
woman with long
legs who knows
she will be older
than her mother
and then finally,
everything dreaded
like the end of
every deep love
kiss, that too
will be done

WHEN IT'S ENOUGH
TO BE IN
THE SAME ROOM

with him. When it's
enough to feel his
skin thru velvet,
my west touching
his east. Of course
the blues will follow
but when it's enough,
the fantasy and the
smell of oozing sap,
cherry snow lasting
longer than he could.
So there won't be
hanky panky, no
thing with blooms
like the Japanese pear.
When on the metro
it's his eyes. When
I'm in danger
of missing my
stop what use to
write a love poem
when it's fantasy. Or
maybe, yes, that is
the right time

BETTER SHE SAID

to put it in a
poem than in
your mouth.
No, it's not
what you're
thinking, not
that I haven't
thought that
myself, not
just that he
is young, that
any ideal I
imagined, would
have imagined,
would have
been his
doppelganger.

It's not only that
he loved my
paintings, how
if I could have
kept him in
storage. Or my
self, waiting
for him to grow
up. But like the
chocolate straw
berry he gave me
and I kept, as
if to keep
him, now it's
time, better in a
poem than
in me

like the way I picked
the cat for her beauty,
her wildness. He is as
stunning and as hard
to hold. A looker and
I'm sure he knows it
as my cat may not.
There is danger behind
the beauty that hooks.
Sure, I've been bitten,
clawed, need drugs to
get over what both have
done. I've got scars.
As with him, with my
cat there's a moment
before she heaves,
gives a little yell or
howl, a cough (Josh
White called it a come
cough, word I hadn't

heard before or later)
There's no chance to
think. If I can grab her,
if she doesn't run
under the bed, dark for
the pale blue silk
Chinese carpet, I can
get her over to the tile
floor or the wood I
can clean up. But if I
miss, as with him, pick
up the wrong clue or
miss it and the beauty
throws up, it's not her
fault, it's something
in her. I forgive her
fast as I suppose, if I
had him, I would and
probably give myself
to scrubbing up his mess

WHEN I WAS NO LONGER

the one he wanted
to be my number 1 fan.
When my poems no longer
made him long
to be young. When he
wanted to read them to a
new lover. When I could
have been one of
them. When it was one of
those another time,
another place dreams. When
just being in his arms
made me blush. When I stopped
doubting there would be
others, felt what
I thought was gone.
When I no longer was
afraid to relax in his arms,
the real was a knife, his
body an invitation
all the women were dying for

WHEN I WAS
NO LONGER
THE OLD PHOTOGRAPHS
HE FELL FOR

that long legged babe in a
bikini on some beach
on white sand he gazed
at dazed. When I was
no longer the sun
he wanted to blind me,
my legs a glue his
wife glowered at,
still was lost in. Then
I was no longer as
addictive as oxycontin,
a narcotic I was his
dealer for. He read poem
after poem, would be
my number 1 fan. Some
days he tracked my
poems to places no one
goes, my words were
seductive as my
legs on the web. In
ballroom he quotes
lines, my metaphors for
tango which was
of course perfect, the
love, the hate, the
staccato where nothing
is as it is for long

WHEN I
NO LONGER KNEW

what to do with
poems that still lured,
when their wildness and
verbs became a mask
for terror. When
the Margaritas did
not do enough, or the
dance teacher's thigh
searing my thigh.
There was nothing
I could do. When I
tried to write poems
of contentment, I
found them a lie. When
fantasy that was a
lie had had more
breath, more fire than
tango and swing,
waltz and bolero and
for romance, lets
say Romantica, the
step I've imagined
doing with one
of the least
real

DREAM OF AN OLD BOYFRIEND

suddenly, he's not only
in my town but in my
bed. It's not what you
think. He's just flown
in from the Midwest
and is exhausted. It's
not exactly a bed, more
of a sofa you can open up
and put sheets on. But I
didn't expect him or
anyone and left it open.
If only he'd let me know
he was coming there'd
be no underwear or baby
doll pajamas flung around
the room. No matter. He
is in town to catch a
thief and maybe worse,
a rapist, murderer. The
local police have flubbed
the case, spit out too
much news so they've
secretly brought in my
ex, so secret I never knew
he was in this week. He
is long and lean. I remember
some of his best qualities
while other lovers fade
away. Neither of us are free
I don't think but it's the
old what goes on in Vegas,
only we're not there,

somewhere else. When
we go out for coffee, yes
we stay dressed—suddenly
he is gone. In minutes I
see him leaping thru alleys,
sprinting up stairs like in
a Law and Order chase.
I'm impressed. His poems
were ok but this is wildly
different. I watch from a
distance. The streets of
people like a scrim. It
almost seems I'm watching
a film where you know he'll
get his man. And will I?
Later back in the flat, we
collapse with a bottle of
wine. We're kind of like
those friends in "Shall we
Kiss" when he's asking her
to help him since he's in
anguish with, for weeks,
no touch and they lie down
a little awkward and I mean
they're friends and never
expected anything like this
but he starts to stroke her
breast, her thighs, under her
clothes and just watching,
well you can imagine in
the dream what is happening

THE CHAMELEON

On Monday, he could
devour me. The next
day, I'm crumbs. He's
the lady killer in one
frame, dunce in the
next. His profile in
Face book, guitar
player, Mona Lisa—
it changes in hours.
Wild to be the most
elusive mystery man
he's a bunny with
waffles and then a
hooded shape in a
sweat shirt with a
globe where a face
should be. He wants
to go places, he wants
to not be tied to
earth, to anyone of
his personas, to
anyone. Sometimes
he's an animal with a
big toy, a skull or Satan.
I've my favorite shot,
movie star looks my
girl friend says. I think
he reminds me of my
first boyfriend and
how I spent afternoons
waiting for him to
call. I'm kind of fond
of him in that black tux

with a furry rabbit
head, enormous ears and
pale fur hands. Imagine
them up and down a body,
or coiling under a quilt
into such ears. When he
is a woman, it doesn't
do much esp not the
one with a telephone
poking from his head or
one that says "dead cat."
I know he loves the *Bicycle
Thief* so of course he'd
want to be the boy in it
or cuddling a dog he does
not own, a sad looking
puppy. But then, his eyes
are sad, too professor like
with glasses Tuesday
maybe with a pipe you
can't see. Maybe he's
dreaming it's Yale, not
the small Texas college
in his town. Give me him
with the hat, not the body
builder in briefs. Not the
robot, not the one that's
just cracked stone: it scares
me. Better the hair slicked
back, a la Astaire and those
eyes that pierce, even
thru each mask

CHAMELEON

after class he taps your
hand as if the curtain's
coming down and a
new face will walk in.
Maybe he sings,
doing an old Fred
Astaire song, doing
the "on the Avenue"
or "Astaire Glide."
Lady Killer someone
hisses, *it's not fair*
to have so much
one woman sighs,
looking. She won't
look straight at him.
Like the sun, it could
blind you. Better
look at the he he was
the last night at Soul
Train, glaring and
cold as if tango made
him nauseous. Better
hope he'll have bad
breath or smell when
he holds you

FOR HIM

I've undressed, not even in
love with what's exposed.
I've pealed off the masks,
left them on the night stand
like jewelry in the tryst we
won't have. I unzip what's
under my hair, the page
is the one place I can
hold him deeper than
the others can. When
he holds me like all the
other dancers, it's rote,
routine. But here, you're
in my claws, I don't leave
a stain, I want, will have you
forever, the one way I can

IMAGINE HIS DAUGHTER

who called while he was
on air, asking where was
the peanut butter. Now she
probably has children of
her own. And the son who
said, when he saw a looker,
he had to jam his fist in
his mouth to not scream,
became a priest. His photo
graphs in a drawer in a house
I rarely go to. They stay
as he never could. Lake blue
eyes the women who tuned into
went mad for like the blue
sweatshirt they fought for.
I painted over the mark he
left on the walls. He filled
poems as he filled me.
Now editors want to change
Vietnam to Iraq. A week
after he told me he
loved, he pulled away,
packed off. Might as
well have been retreating
in to the jungle. Not you,
not your fault he insisted,
crazed. It's old news but
those words jar, a knife,
tho he's still dead

WHEN THE CAT HOWLS

nudges you, it's like
a woman down on her
knees, rubbing herself
against you. She's got
new food and water.
What does she want?
Isn't she like a woman
with a good man of her
own longing, inconsolable
as the cat? Something
under her hair sucks her
toward bad boys. She's
got her claws out for
him. She's putting her
deepest purr on the line.
Someone ought to put
her in a cage for her
own good. Someone's
got to let her know
what's what

WHEN I HEARD HE WAS DEAD

it stung, not that it
wasn't long enough
ago for the cat I had
then to have litters
and litters of kittens
but that years I hadn't
been with him
Even before we met
he'd reviewed my
books in the best
places, wrote blurbs,
never let me down.
He was as close to
my mother's age as
mine, the oldest man
I ever dated. He
appeared just as I
learned my husband
was running around.
My husband told
him to call me then
showed up with a bottle

of red wine the night
of that date. I opened
new polka dot sheets
with a yellow border,
past, now, being
rags. I bought blue
berry muffins. When I
went to the art colony
he gave me a bottle of
scotch I think the
cleaning woman slugged
and sent me a ticket from
Europe to join him.
When I went back to
try to make things work
with my husband, he
married a woman he
met three weeks before.
It must have been
convenient that her
name was my name

THE ONE WITH MAHOGANY EYES, CURLS AND LASHES ANY GIRL WOULD HAVE DIED FOR

I think of his new leather
coat my cat scratched
that night November
escaped, ran thru the
prickly chestnuts and
Peter ran after him.
Of course there was
more than his flash of
temper. I wouldn't be
thrilled with claws of dog
bites even on an old
rain coat but I remember
his prickliness, how intent
he was on my wanting
to have babies (which I
didn't) His sister dated so
many men I had, even
my cousin's husband but
that had nothing to do
with him. I remember how
he always wanted a blow
job. Little else

WITH ONE IT WAS BASEBALL

long and lean, somehow a parole
officer. I mean the baseball books
sold but I guess the novels? I'm not
sure. He was pleasant at the art
colony but I saw slivers of a military
Nazi like few moves. Nothing you'd
run from, nothing you'd call belligerent
but when you're in a mansion, a few
drinks before dinner, a walk thru a
garden of lilacs, a little lunch brought
to your studio in a basket, someone
to clean your room and bring new
towels. In the real world where I had
another boyfriend, it was different.
With no warning he showed up in my
town. Just back from my downstate
lover, unpacking and washing my
hair, he started knocking on the door.
My silence didn't discourage him.
I waited an hour, my heart pounding
while he banged. Then I thought it was
safe only to find ladders pressed up
against the upstairs windows, rescue
workers, fire men, police, wild to
know if I was ok. With his parole office
connections, he tried to track me in
various towns. He could call cops
in a town when he thought I would be
there. This got old. The knock on the
door in the night. My real boyfriend
didn't go for the drill and the parole
officer baseball writer finally backed
off until years later at a ranch in
California he showed up. I was touring

with a film maker and when I agreed
to go out for a drink, said she would
have to come too. I saw a flash of rage, it
had that door banging craziness, the
insistence of firemen peering
in my window and suddenly I
could imagine him doing something
not connected to playing ball with
a baseball bat

WITH HIS FLUTE
AND HIS STRIPED CLOAK

and his British accent
and a sweet con way.
Not my type but some
how there I was, driving
him to New Haven.
A chauffeur, a hooker.
I probably bought
him food. Yearly he'd
leave his wife and babies
and pick up easy money
on a cross US tour,
picking up women to
take him wherever he
wanted from state to
state or in bed. He left a
trail of unpaid phone
bills later to India,
Alaska, Egypt to Siam
and Timbuktu,
confident he could pull
off what was needed

THERE WERE MANY
SCARS AROUND HIS HEART

maybe why he was so
driven to make so many
in others! At the art colony,
under my door, "You'd
be pretty if you didn't
try to be." That edge, in
his poems. But then, he
killed a wasp in my room,
brought me carnations.
When he came from
England for surgery or
sex I took the train to the
Village or met him at
the plane. The last time he
seemed old and I was
heart broken over
another. Late October
I think and the leaves dead
as I knew what had been
between us

I SAW HIM
ACROSS THE SWANS

before I touched him:
the Boston Gardens, a free
concert. Something stayed
so at the art retreat—to
have him across the table
and later in my bed near
the octagonal tub seemed
unreal. His "Baby Won't You"
a drug, his fingers on the
strings, foreplay. No matter
his last lover said "you
mean you think I enjoy this?"
and it stung so he wondered
if he could ever again.
Those June nights blur
but not the waiting for him,
so many women hypnotized
by his blues. I hated cigars
but for that short time
it didn't matter. Or the rum
he spilled in my Maverick
or Woodstock nights he
played until dawn, drinking
and hollering and singing
and laughing, me the only
one not a music star—
I keep the sketches he did
of me like sacred relics
and the one a famous
cartoonist did of us
together and play his records,
feel him singing in the stained
glass room just to me

SOME LOVES

one love, the opposite of
handsome. So funny.
But the second night
at the artist dorm I
held him in the bracelet
of my thighs as if
I could. Was it his
voice? His stories?
How he made me feel
everything in the end
would come out better?
Colorado, Niskayuna,
Virginia, and Colorado
again under his mobile
of was it dinosaurs
or cats? How could I
not remember or
believe now he is
disabled and I never
knew. I think it was the
last time he said he
thought he loved me,
days it seemed his
cats were my cats

ONE MAN

took me to breakfast,
might as well have been
a million years ago

Someone who was supposed
to meet me didn't. My
hair thicker and

darker, perfect skin
tho I didn't know. A
decade ago he saved me at

an Above Paradise reading
on the west coast. He was
a looker. He seemed to care

I couldn't remember, did I
sleep with him in some
abandoned year? and

then near the Everglades
he was there, with a look, a
way that said somehow

we had. Even with his
woman walking thru the
park with Florida flowers

perfuming the night, some
intimacy, some talk, some
hush as if we knew too

much about each other.
These last
months he writes me more:

how I didn't eat any
breakfast, just wasn't
hungry and in the last note

this week, days nothing
good has happened, his
freeze frame of me:

on the bus stunning
he writes you were stunning,
wildly stunning

then you were gone

160

SOMETIMES ON THE METRO
FOR NO REASON

I imagine your thoughts
flying to me. I think of
how they say two photons
fired thru a slit stay paired
forever. As if they could
chose this. I'm not asking
for much. Just lets call
it photon tango. That one
place someone who isn't
you can be as long as
the CD holds out. So close
for a wrong step. Thigh
blood braiding as much one
almost as with a lover in bed

OTHER LOVERS

carry you up to the
garnet bedroom with
your boots on. Some
rub chocolate all over
then steal your Kennedy
silver dollars when you
leave him the key.
Some never hear you
even if they aren't
deaf. Other men say
because of a leg they
lost in Iraq, they can
get closer to you. When
they say they love,
it's almost the last
thing they say except
"it's not you, it's me."
Turn your knuckles
raw knocking on his
door: sex will be
great but it always
will be over

SOME LOVERS: FOREPLAY

e mail is stupendous
but when you meet in
Venezuela, just a dry
kiss. When he doesn't
write for half a year
you imagine him dead.
Or on a stranded beach
in Big Sur or kidnapped
by aliens. When he
writes you save every
word on your hard drive.
One lover taught me
what men did in prison,
things I'll never see
again. Some are startlingly
gorgeous, exotic as
a Lamborghini everybody stares
at but they are too expensive
to keep, always falling
apart, leaving you stranded,
having to be lugged home
in your arms

SOME LOVES

hitch across country
to get into your pants,
astonished they are
the first one. Some
will make a dash
exit in the middle
of the night on your
birthday hissing you
are too needy and
then, for decades,
gasp, in letters, then
e mail, how your
body enchanted as
no others had. He'll
want to meet in
Paris or Madrid.
Some are in for the
chase, see you as
prey, a wild doe they
wouldn't know
what to do with
except shoot

SOME LOVERS

ask if you'd marry
them if they asked but
don't ask. Leave a note
on your door: they
want to catch up
(which means a blow
job) Some think
you can help them
with their poetry.
Some think you are
your poems. Some
that you fantasize and
want the most, can't
be seduced, not
even in dreams. You
give them what no
one else can in poems
where they will always
be fit and young
and they give you
dark blues

SOME LOVERS

are only hot on
e mail. You must have
known men like
that. But then, after
we both fly halfway
across the country,
only a dry kiss.
Others shove your
cat off the bed.
You imagine you'll
get the same treatment.
Still, it doesn't follow
if one saves a stray
diabetic cat and
cuddles and loves him,
that he'll do the same
by you. And what
to make of the lover
who says he can't find
anything wrong with
you, says you're up there
in his "top ten girl
friends." Or the one
who was so stingy he
used his tea bag
12 times, opened a
box of cookies his
mother sent him,
munched away but
didn't offer you one.
Some lovers are
Tuesday might lovers,
a fuck, not a bad one,
a cup of tea and
he's gone.

OTHER LOVERS

want you to touch
there and there, some
hardly want you
near them. Some
expect you to score
cocaine or weed
tho you don't use
them, substitute
nutmeg that keeps
you in a daze. Some
marry you and still
won't touch you.
Some try but can't
really touch you.
Others haunt after it
is over, their voice
on radio air. Others
have hearts that
aren't right, some
are heart broken.
Some break your heart

SOME MEN
THAT AREN'T QUITE LOVERS

one was a looker, then
suddenly, on the steps up
to the dorm, pulled out his
penis. Four years later,
even more handsome,
he pulled a "Ronnie
Sussman" in the lobby of
the college dorm. Some pass
out on your couch and
you can't get rid of them.
One offered me a job,
grabbing my crotch. When
I pushed him away he
took back his offer. One
said he was joining the army.
I ought to do the dirty,
that it was the patriotic
thing to do. Some try to
hypnotize you, say they'll
count back from ten
and you'll let him do what
he wants and you'll forget it.
One saw my picture in
Rolling Stone, asked if I had a
Jewish nose, said I looked
like Dylan's girlfriend.
He wanted to send me plane
fare. He thought since he
was an ex Bird, I'd be
thrilled to have him judge
me nude, test me out. Then
like another he told me
he put on the next plane back,
be happy to let him walk
all over me

ANOTHER SORT OF LOVER

One was the last man in the
world I would have wanted.
I turned TV off when he did
the sports news. No one
could have less in common
with me. A date to a play,
the only reason I went. I
got a few poems out of the
night at the motel with hearts
on the ceiling and mirror
he passed out under. Some
where, a warm up jacket I
wore and scorched years later
when the power went out
and the Challenger exploded.
I doubt he read anything more
than the sports page. Yet he
wanted to marry me, live
a life of bliss watching the
Yankees train in their winter
home in Florida, spend the
rest of the year at football
or basketball games
and hockey

EVEN MORE LOVERS

One I slept with to
make the one I really
wanted jealous. He
represented me in
court and then wanted
to present me with
his penis. He lived at
home but one weekend
his parents away, he
took me for the
night. He was cute but
I didn't care, especially
when he tried to stick
vegetables in strange
places. I wanted his
law partner. I never
stopped wanting him.
That was the last of a
few nights I wanted
to want him

THOSE LOVERS

some, lets say the first,
you stop eating for,
call at the last moment.
If you are 13 you're sure
you can't live without
them. Or you work on
science projects fever-
ishly, aching for the
phone. Some join the
Navy, send you cheap
Cuban coins from there,
S.W.A.K. on the box.
His uniform makes you
heady. Weeks of kisses
in his navy blues and
then on leave, he shrugs
when asked if you should
wear a stole and never
again is heard from.
Some take you out in
a field, then upstairs in
the hotel where you let
him peal off spray rhine
stone earrings and the
stretchy wool dress
with net and sparkles.
And when you don't
let them peel your hymen
from what's still holding
it, don't call again. Some
you never cared for but
needed a date for some prom.
Others are so insistent it's
easy to waste a night or two
with them. The ones that

are too shy to call, you
feel their eyes burning
thru you. Some would be
lovers call from the Vatican
or Notre Dame say they have
their vows but would you send
something that's been close to you
like your un-washed underwear

PASSING
ARLINGTON
CEMETERY

Sunday, the metro, this
late summer. The tangle,
stations shut when a
man leaped from the
platform. Cool and dry
enough for my hair
not to curl like child's
hand curls about a finger.
But September curls
back to that first time I
heard his voice. Upstate.
Enough years back that
his daughter, calling the
all night radio show:
she couldn't find peanut
butter, is old enough to
have a daughter her age
then, visiting her father.
It was an afternoon, clear
like today driving up
the Helderg mountains
to do a reading, when I
heard his voice. Not the
first man I fell for before
I met him but something
in his voice, what he was
saying, I knew I had
to have him

AUGUST SARATOGA

the arms of young girls
tan and taut, breasts

curve in their pale
summer dresses

laughing. The wine
glasses lose their ruby

When I was as
stunning, I had no idea

These magnets, lilac
flowers, wet lips

and sleek hair
leaning across the table

like young girls
practicing, kissing

the mirror

THE MAD GIRL THINKS OF JOSEPH CONRAD'S
HEART OF DARKNESS, THE HORROR

lights up the hisses
after a barrage or
"stupid ass hate"
and "stupid bitch"
If there was sun,
she wouldn't see it.
Monday, Tuesday,
a black hole. On
the metro, families
clutch children like
jewels. She knows
someone must have
held her like a rare
gift too but last
night's sleeping
pills left her groggy.
Sylvia and the
sludge of the kitchen,

of drugs is as clear
to her mood tho often
she's become what she
is called: slut, cold.
Say her waltz is lovely
and she'll float off
the floor but one
sneer, one "follow me
you jerk" and she's a
disaster, unable to do
the step she's done
for ages, unable to
think of anything lighter
than Conrad's heart on
Heart of Darkness,
knows she feels at the
center it is the horror,
the horror

THE MAD GIRL IS TOO HARD ON HERSELF

an extra pound and
she used to want to
cut flesh from her
belly. Lucky she
isn't a cutter (except
in her poems.) If she
sliced, when things
felt dicey, she'd be
be as scarred as
marks on distressed
wood, hammered
veal calves, bloodied
and beat. If she
misses a dance step
she can't forgive
herself or sleep, is
so wild of course the
next time too she
won't have it. Only
a lullaby at one barre
has rocked her back
to when she wasn't
guilty or wrong or
to blame. To camou-
flage her anger and
grief, she buys clothes
the way someone else
might booze or eat
chocolate. She can't
stop ordering velvets
she doesn't need,
mini skirts in lace
and leather, silver
lame as if what
sparkles when she
won't, like light
from a dead planet,
will make you believe
everything inside
her isn't dead

It's not the first time
she dreams of her,
Vincent with her velvet
and wildness. Horse-mad
too. No, not just her
being a young beauty
from the wrong part of
a small town. She
doesn't have Edna's
big boobs, but her hair
is longer, wavier. But
today she wants to read
about Edna's last flame,
the young lover she
turned herself to crisp
on, the one who adored,
threw himself at her
knees, a supplicant
entranced by her
words. The mad girl
knows what that's like.
She had her own
gasping, bleating "her
number 1 fans," and
then suddenly he is off
into sci fi. Or was it
Japanese films? She
thinks of Millay
noting what sagged,
how her perfect skin
wasn't. "Kind of blue"
pings in her head.
Like Millay, she'd
prefer the stable
husband there, to be
there for her when
the world seemed too

much. Somehow to
soothe her and hold her
when dreams knifed
the night. Someone
whose steadiness was,
someone to bring
her oranges and valium.
Someone who'd stay
when the baby lovers
vanish. She thinks of
Millay burning candles
at both ends, feeling like
a hooker when she
got up to read: paid for
getting undressed,
getting nude, getting
naked. But today it's
that ache Millay felt at
not being the adored
beauty, magnetic to
editors, publishers,
readers: all men. Gone
like the red in her hair.
The mad girl's was
more fiery too and the
men wouldn't stop
falling. But it's Vincent's
last terrible lover, the
one she turned into
sonnets that tear out
your heart the mad girl
shivers at, painting a
last brush stroke to
finish the one she longed
for too long, as if to
use him as she feels
he did her

THE MAD GIRL REMEMBERS WHEN SHE STOOD
BEHIND THE GIRL WHO'D BE A MODEL
THEN DUMPED BEING TOO OLD AT 19

how she longed for
Sally Smith's long
long legs, thighs
that weren't always
kissing each other
but let light thru. The
mad girl hated her
fat thighs on benches
for basket ball games.
Even at six she scowled
in the mirror seeing
her soft fat thighs
in a bathing suit,
belly she didn't
believe wouldn't always
betray her. She
remembers being
weighed in front of the
class and how Mr.
Dewey belted out
the numbers, how she
weighed more than
most of the boys in the
class. "Chubbette"
an uncle with a clothes
store nagged, "the
regular pre teen skirts
won't fit you." But the
mad girl refused. She
would, even pared down,
lie on her bed to zip
jeans at least one
size too small, refuse
to wear anything over
size 0. But it's the early
days when kids yelled
"fat" out the window,
worse to her than "kike"
or "two eyes" or "kinky hair"
or "book worm." Now she
wishes she could dance
depression out of her,
write this one man
into so many poems in
real life she'll be too
numb to have feelings
about him, paint him as
dull. Her legs no longer
smack each other as if
applauding or kissing
but hold the little that
is left of her, so light,
almost air. She danced
with the one she
chose, he'd hold her up
and she could easily
follow wherever
he wanted her to go

THE MAD GIRL'S STUNNED WALKING UP
FROM THE METRO

there, on a bench, with
his sack of clothes
or maybe food
scavenged out of
some dumpster.
A man sits on a park
bench. He's got a
black knit cap on tho
it's close to 90 in
the shade. A heavy
brown coat, and his
hair, dark and wavy,
hangs in long curls
not just to the side
walk but sprawls
over the pavement.
She thinks Medusa,
or Rapunzel. Long
snakes of hair and
maybe in his sack,
baby somethings
he's intent on getting

gone. Or maybe, she
thinks, he's a male
Rapunzel watching
the young kiss in front
of Starbucks, dream-
ing even if he has not
had a bath, even if
there's weeks of earth
under his nails and
his hair smells of the
alleys he's slept in
because they've never
seen anything quite
like these rivers of
hair, this hair octopus,
just there, in the middle
of Silver Spring because
it is so unearthly they
might, like the mad girl,
climb that fuzzy rope
who knows how they
will come back from

one, who got bald, never
taking it off, maybe even
to shower. Dark stormy
eyes. A pretty boy,
pretty much a jerk. I
learned when he told
half of Hillel I let him
do what his wife
wouldn't except for
Christmas. I never had
a man with a base
ball cap backwards
no cowboy brims
but in the bookstore
in a Pork Pie—is that
what it was? A slouchy
look half pulled
over one eye. He took
me to his hotel to show
me video equipment.
Such long legs. I tripped

in boots meant more
for the dance floor.
Even one terrible hat.
July he wore it and he
suddenly seemed old.
And then last night,
how silly to think I'd
been inoculated
against, that time and
space took care of
caring, that with too
many floors dissolving
under me it would be
electric to just share
space and if only it was
that hat, a panama with
the smoldering eyes
under it and that grin,
that small wave. Why do
the bad boys always charm?

LETTING YOU FADE
FROM THE POEMS

gone, the way clouds
skim over the moon's
face. With you, it was
always illusion. It's the
way in this light, milk
weed pods explode
in the dark honey of
night. Small flowers,
ghost flowers,
dissolving like words
that shouldn't have
mattered, shadowy as
deer shifting thru
apples, then the gray
fox, stunning,
haunting as
gone eyes

ON NIGHTS
BEFORE
YOU SAID YES

would she have been
nothing if she was
just wrong?

soon trains
dissolve

driving the
dead back up

MIDSUMMER NIGHT

the moon's face
almost full
silvering between
clouds. Stars
dissolve. A single
firefly. In this
pale light,
as with you,
outlines blur. I
can't make out
tiger lilies
opening, onyx
spots startling as
your black eyes,
a thick musk
in blackness crowds
the fence past
the rose
dogwood balls

AFTER THE LAST MOTEL

it was taking a cruise
all the way to the wharves
toward mad nights
and flaking away

The smell of her coats
at that grease and mustard motel

but she'll like what's gone
more. She fingers her
lips, plunges in nights
where her face ends

even takes the smack ups
like re-runs

WHEN IT
DISAPPEARS,
WHEN IT WAS
JUST THERE

then it isn't. It's
like a lover who,
the day after he
adores you says
no, "it's not you,
it's me" and no
banging your
knuckles to blood
on his door will
let you in. When it
was just where you
could put your hands
on and suddenly,
stabbingly, isn't,
like a child gone
missing, a cat that
always slept in
the cove of your
body, suddenly gone
and this not-there
takes up the space in
your heart, the
what-isn't howls.
When you wake up
it's the first thing
you think of.
You try to dream
where it would be
but you can't sleep

THEN

Deirdre feels trapped
in the driftwood docks

she's made out of
it, night bleached

leaving it his

LATER

tree girl stays where
the wild shadows are

she can't escape

the slithering,

that final stain

AFTER THE LAST POST

Dolphin girl remembers
the tangy chlorine

ambience. You
pulled against it.

His charm, lightning,
pulled you in

EVEN HIS SON

an array of masks.
He's Kong and Mr.
Dinosaur. Then a
bear. Of course his
father is never the
same person. You
might as well be
meeting a new lover
or father. He's brittle,
he's a bear himself.
He loves but then
it's the old knife
eyes, the sheik who
doesn't find any
of the twenty in his
harem right: the artist,
the dancer, the mobster
in his black and white
shoes, his black and
white heart, his black
and white mood.
The warmth that
slithers in, startling
as a gray fox darts
across green as if it
was your skin, wild
then gone

Pictures

HOLIDAY BLUES

when I read my sister's
words on a blog, they
could have been mine.
So close, as we are
not. The exact words,
as we haven't any.
December grows
darker fast. What
was, a rain of strangers
dissolving from a
train window I'll never
see again

ON A DAY
THE MAD GIRL FEELS
SHE IS A WOMAN
IN AN EDWARD HOPPER
PAINTING

Staring into nothing.
It's her with a cigarette
dangling tho she does
not smoke, a joint
of sadness. Someone
could come, it
hardly matters. Her
clothes could dissolve
in a breath. Or
maybe she's already
had men, is finished
with men who had
her, turned their
face to the sheets,
checked his watch.
Her breasts hurt
from how he held
on so tight, her skin
holds your brand
and it's leaked
deeper.

THE MAD GIRL HAS
NO INTEREST
IS NOT DYING TO TRAVEL

She doesn't want to
eat wild pig in
Poland, drink 120
proof vodka. She
doesn't want
a cruise. What she
is starved for
isn't on the table.
She's seen
enough stained
glass. Every
thing she looks at
is thru her own
stained glass

GRAY SUNDAY
ON THE METRO

Fog drifts into
my head. Some
thing's lost as
3 of the goslings,
there and not
there. Too many
streets where
everything I
remember enters
me. No shadows,
no color, only
some velvet swatch
for what I don't
need, like
your player
words add color
and like you,
are too expensive,
irresistible

I HAVE LOST THE FIRE

just thinking of you
the flame you brought
in your voice and hair.
Something different
bites into the river of
May where once your
fingers along my spine
were all that mattered
I am forgetting
that touch, that
long embrace I
could have let be the
last thing I breathed
This strangeness
moves into my
dreams my wrists.
How could this wild
bright May, azaleas
in more shades
than there are words
numb the longing
in my wrists. Of course
I lie. Just your
face in the room,
a comfort, just
imagining your
fingers indelible on
skin—muscle
memory that chills
like the falls
outside my lilac
room, rainbow
spray I was lured
by and, like you,
terrified to
plunge into

TATTOO

Sometimes all those
with tattoos pierced on
perfect skin will not
be what they were.
A flabby arm,
sagging nipples.
Someone will pass
out in a bar or
grocery store and
where you can't see
a heart fading,
blurring, "Edie" or
"Tom" hardly
legible, some
hieroglyph haunting
as blue tattoos,
a blue stain, what
longing for you
has scarred

TONIGHT
ON THE METRO
I FELT LIKE A NUN

they must imagine, I
mean even if they'll
never see what's
mysterious as the
mystical. Could
they not wonder
about that bracelet
of dark hair around
the bone. Or even
wonder about hair
around the other bone.
Even married to
Jesus wouldn't
they maybe even
dream what's under
some man's dark
jeans or cotton
as I can't help but
feel the outline
deep in tango,
so close bodies
move as one

LATER
IN A DREAM
IN A HOUSE

of snow, where I
feel as lost as last
night, not even our
eyes connected.
You'd been more
close as if our
bodies could
press into each
other or maybe
press the other
away. But your
hand lies against
mine, it's just
there and I don't
move

ON THE BLUE DAY

whatever isn't, hangs
like the smell of
cooking, a smear over
Monday. The daughter
I would, I know, let
writing go for, the man
with cold lake eyes,
December blues.
Surely my daughter,
after the giggles
and smiles, would have
sunk into sadness too,
terror. But if I had
her I could hold her,
bring her a cup of
warmth, rub her
back, keep her
close as sapphire
and cobalt wash over
us, the hues most
startling, most
beautiful, the most
iridescent when light
passes over them

IF THERE IS ANDEAN MUSIC
AT THE TOP OF
THE METRO STAIRS

and the dentist
doesn't find anything wrong,

the pansies, beaten
down by icy rain

glow by the time I
set out for home,

yellow, mauve and
purple. Some

where else, a woman
dies after three days, her

flesh burned, her
baby dead in the ashes

so this Thursday, still
a little flu dazed

in my heavy parka, the
hood turning voices eerie

I'm ready to dream
back to Vienna

TATIANA

on a night of lights,
on a night the wind
blew cedar past the ocean,
Tatiana, a name I would
chose for myself,
close to Gitana, gipsy,
but softer. Her beauty,
wildness. Tatiana, the
mystery still unfolds.
Taunted, something in
the air a lure. Some
unearthly leap over the
moat. Something
twisting, the pattern
no human could see. She
was a beauty, a savage
beauty. Some adrenalin
rush, she was claws
and tears burning. She
was astonishing
until she wasn't

TATIANA

not sea glass
but the raging waves

now, no grass
or sun

no lemon wind
blown north

her eyes, the color of lemons

Her muscles rippled
in the light

burning, burning

TATIANA

some blood
inside the
fence, a
shoe

muscles coiled,
think of the tiger
seeing a dangling leg

maybe, a
leg like
meat chunks,
becoming meat chunks

the tiger
being a tiger

"THAT CRAZY MAN
ON THE TRAIN"

a girl with a butterfly
on her tawny skin
laughs, "he ought to
get himself into bed
and sleep it away."
From Dupont metro
center, waving some
thing in his left hand
and shouting out
"lights," or maybe,
"blights"—a hand
grenade, a notebook,
some bomb camou-
flaged as a book. A
woman near him
was laughing, a good
sign I guess. Maybe
they've been at a
party or just went out
and had too much
to drink. I like that
better than supposing
something in what
he's shaking has
something to do with
how he's jerking
his hand up a la Heil
Hitler or maybe
he's just wondering
if somehow on the
metro there's a men's
room and maybe he
really needs it

HOW TO WRITE
A NOT GUSHY
SENTIMENTAL
WHAT WOULD
YOU CALL IT
POEM?

even if it's just his hip
against your hip, how
he touches your velvet,
turns the drab day of
rain to jewels. Just
remember even in
fantasy you are one
of his harem. Sure, his
eyes are drugs. You,
but you know I mean
I, am scooped up, it
feels like he's an animal
carrying me in the
protection of his mouth,
not sure I won't
be swallowed

THE SOMEHOW I CAN'T GET THE DREAM RIGHT
POEM, MAYBE BECAUSE I DON'T WANT IT OVER

when I couldn't get him,
have him, couldn't get
him out of fantasy.
When I was in the car
or at the barre in ballet.
When I knew. Not like
I could say he has left
the building and let
him blur seeing him
almost each night at
ballroom, his thigh
sliding up my thigh
in a class or two a
week. Like alcohol
to someone drying

out. Awake, nothing
was as it could be.
To escape in sleep
was hardly enough
and then as magnolias
began, after the
margaritas, after
stinging needles in
bad dreams, suddenly
I'm as summery in
as a blooming magnolia.
My legs have lost
their scars, my hair
is thicker, red.

THE MAD GIRL
ONLY FEELS ALIVE
WHEN SHE IMAGINES
HE FEELS
THE ELECTRICITY
SHE HALF CAMOUFLAGES

an even more dangerous tango,
more subtle, wild.
Her words sucked on his body.
It was all danger. She
could feel him on another
sheet, the touch,
searing, a brand. She
could feel he could feel
her, she was burning. She wanted
to move more beautifully
for him, wanted
to dance like her verbs. Magnolia
snow. She can feel him
as she writes this. Teak eyes
ghost dancing, a needle
in the heart

THE MAD GIRL FEELS HIM IN HER FINGERS, HER SKIN

that almost pain chill,
a needle in her arm.
If you haven't felt
it you don't know
her. She wants more
and more. Wants
to audition for
flamenco at 2 AM
in a sketchy
part of town,
would break up
your family if she
could but only
for the lava
inside her. "Foxy
Lady" they yelled
at Muscle Beach.
Some days they

still do. What she
aches for is elusive
as a man made
of snow. Her first
poems had that
image in them. What
was intoxicating
and then melting
quickly, snow
flaked beauty, there
and then not. Now
only she warms
the place filled by
her body. All
she is missing and
starved for is
what she
can't have

DREAM OF FOGGED OVER DESTINATIONS,
A TRAIN STATION, LANGUAGE I NEVER LEARNED

Maybe it's Gard de Norde.
Maybe I overslept. Or I
was on a flight I don't
remember. It's early, gray,
a snow slush grey. The
mist is so thick I could
not find your face and of
course you're not there.
You're the destination
I only had fantasies about,
the dream escape that
could never not be a let
down. This is so unlike
my first trip alone to
Colorado: huge suitcase
(I never don't drag too
much of what I can't use
around—closets and
notebooks bulging. Rods
crack and I can't shut the
door—years at college
and art colonies sneaking
thru French doors,
embarrassed, my arms
bulging with heaps of
silk and gold). Excessive,
obsessive, forgetting,
spilling the bottle of vodka,
how it slid thru my arms,
a give away like poems
about the one of course
I can't hold. Maybe he is
what I'm stalking but
without a ticket, I'm
stranded. No make up,
colorless as the thick air,
the only color is the blue
of the train's moan,
leaving, leaving,
bluer than blue

HE WOULDN'T MIND
IF I WROTE ABOUT HIM

when it's a kaleidoscope of
shifting ebony and ruby
glass. When he presses
his hips into mine, of
course he has to, it's
tango. When the verbs
are fiction. When the
dead strawberry has
been trashed. When his
"and you know I am good"
still makes me shiver
and I spray rose where
I know he'll touch.
Too often, across the
room, his look startles
like the calf torso coming
out slick and black, legs
crossed over one another,
head last. His eyes,
that wobbly calf's blunt
mouth sucking on me

THE MAD GIRL
DRENCHES HER FINGERS
WITH ROSE

tea rose, tuber
rose, Bulgarian
and white heir-
loom rose. She
wants to leave
her scent, brand
the one she can
only hold for
a moment. Pale
rose, white rose,
Damask. She is
wild to have him
remember. Maybe
he'll smell her,
then dream there
could be more.

NO SLEEP AND
TOO MANY PILLS

water pools in the
roses. My head's
under water in the
rouge blues. So
it's not raining
but it will be. This
blue Friday, a
roach I can't
escape without
a wall of them
burying me

WALKING TO THE METRO

ten days from the day
of least light. All
day the temperature
near 60, geese circling
the pond as I think
how its never been so
long since I watched the
last streak of the sky's
persimmon. A year from
when many were
wondering where the
Derby winner would go,
that warm spell that
seemed to go on
forever as what seemed
so hopeful wouldn't

HOLIDAY BLUES

the dark rain on
the way to the airport.
Mist and sleep. The
thick slog of morning
after Plath's stink
of cooking. He says
I'm angry, it isn't
working. Blue rises
thru clouds. Engine
moan. A bottle of
pills on the nightstand
would glisten more
than any strung lights.
Only what I can do

A CHRISTMAS CARD
FROM 1974

arrives with a 1 cent stamp
somewhere in Kansas.
Only the sister is alive
as mine no longer is
to me. No sister, no
daughter to bring a cup
of something warm on a
bad day, sit near her as
my own mother did.
I wanted to help her grow
older, not feel so alone.
Or, find, like this
card, it was too late for
what mattered, if
I had her

FLU DAZED, TOO EARLY
ON THE METRO

tie-dyed sky still,
the black antler branches

burning from quilts,
staggering to feed the cats

Is this mauve, still horizon
salve for this

too early trip to the dentist?
Wedged in near a

woman who won't fling
her body as if

she owned all space,
scrunched to the aisle.

Who here won't float in
sickness. These blues, the

coughing 7:30 on the
Orange line, coughs,

sneezes, the day's paper
in the aisle, old snow.

Shivering in a turtle
neck and two heavy sweat

shirts and an LL Bean
parka for more degrees cold

than I can imagine

FLU TRAIN

this time I'm the one
coughing, wedged
between a man
who takes up all the
space and those stand-
ing in the aisles. The
train gets colder,
stalled at West Falls
Church. More pile on.
I'm still aching,
longing to be back
under blue quilts.
I want this trip to the
dentist over, want
there to be nothing
wrong. I want to
be in a cocoon
of warm blankets
with someone to bring
me pineapple and
cherry juice in a tall
thin cup with a
glass straw

FLU ON AN EARLY TRAIN

crumpled as an old
document. As I go
underground I think
of trees upside down,
the branches roots.
What I can't see is
most with me: those
dreams of being
underwater, orange
feet of geese their
only sun

imagine him in the stacks,
probably white hair—if he's
not, would you notice the
difference? A man who
blends in with the library
gloom, one who remembers
card catalogues. A man
who wouldn't hold you up
in an alley but can't resist an
old map of Madagascar or
maybe one with figures and
pale washes of ink. It could
be San Luis Obispo or Sierra
Leone. He's like a child
molester, the sort of man
you wouldn't expect with his
urges and obsessions. Maybe he
focuses on maps related to
exploration and colonization
of the Americas. Or maybe he
lusts for Timbuktu. Very bad
acts he knows. A man others
describe as professorial, a New
England Yankee type at home
in the world where luxury cars,
amounts of money are spent to
indulge historical obsession.
He sold the maps so long some
one had it in their gut that he
was stealing. He did it twenty
years until he dropped an X-
Acto blade on the floor of a
library reading room, a 390
year old map on him with a
picture of early colonist John
Smith worth about 50 grand.
It was missing from a book
in the library

ON THIS
JUST SPRING GRAY
SUNDAY RAIN
WALK TO THE METRO

Overnight it seems
the leaves have leafed out.
Red crystals of maple,
green hands

The branches are stretching
out of their bodies,
braids of light

dipping into the
blue shoulders of
Nutley Pond

This week I escaped
the dark river of loss

and the ordinary glistens,
blue berries in a blue bowl,
the cat stalking the gray

a stillness with no one
shouting or crying

tho I know it won't
always be this way

SIX DAYS
BEFORE MY MOTHER'S
BIRTHDAY

some noise in the woods,
these weeks, thinking
so long of her.
Trillium in the pachysandra
near where I planted
the ones I dug up
the Mother's Day after
her mother died.
Those flaring white petals
half knocked out by
a snow plow. Now
bending into dark earth
as if replanting that
sun north of Middlebury.
I lived alone, wasn't
sure I wouldn't always
but couldn't imagine her
not at the edge of
the phone or
waiting for any word
from me. The cat
she never saw curls in
the tub, she's
found sun in unlikely
places. For my
mother, my voice was
that brightness

DREAM OF THE ROOTING HORSE CHESTNUT AND
THE READING I SHOULD HAVE NEVER TAKEN,
SHOULD HAVE CANCELED BUT THERE'S A HUGE
CROWD STILL, I'M TERRIFIED AND ON TOP OF THAT,
I'M TOPLESS

Somehow, I've planned to drive to a reading
states away and I don't really drive. Oh, I've had
a license since I was 16 but since I moved to DC
and Virginia, I take metro every where, only
drive a few blocks. I must have been mad,
totally insane to not plan on a train or bus or
plane. I barely drive to get my hair trimmed, was
I hypnotized or drugged to agree? If my mother
could drive with me, if I wasn't so terrified but
she's having surgery and there's no way she would
or could change that date to go with me to this
poetry reading. I'm freaking. I've lost the phone
number of the contact. It's way too late to make
other plans but somehow a screen flashes up with
hundreds of people waiting in seats, waiting
for me, irresistible as certain eyes and smiles. I
don't see how I can get there. Suddenly I realize I
am in public half naked, nothing on top and dive
for my suitcase where I pull on what I can to
cover me. I've a top with three sleeves. I put 2
that don't work on one arm, the least of the day's
weirdness. Then I find a chestnut, the word I'd
typed the night before, the color of eyes on another
alluring place I can't get to. Then, I see the shiny
mahogany glow is rooting, growling pale
hair roots into my skin

WITHOUT A BOOK
ON THE METRO

to escape. I'm stuck
again, drawn back to you.
What woman isn't. 3/4ths
of the class is in love with
you and that's only the
women. I want to forget
the another- life, another-
time crap. We aren't, we
don't, we won't.
Altar boy, heart throb,
charmer. So you didn't
finish college, think
publishing books is
great while I'd burn
my books (well, no
probably not but give up
something else that
matters) to dance like
you do or the women
you hold. We're each in
love but with what
we don't have

WILLOWS YELLOWING

he says he and
his wife see each
other so rarely,
they really ought
to have a date.

I think of the women
he holds all week
in his arms. I think
of his arms when I
should be typing.

Reading a book on
the metro I try to
escape, try to imagine
the warm quilt waiting,
the cat maybe dreaming
of flayed fish.

And why can't the
one who'll curl into
my hair and want to
hold me be less
real than ghosts of you

THE FIRST YEAR
I DIDN'T SEE
THE WILD PLUMS

my favorite, go from
swollen, to rouge
to lip then explode
in flesh blossoms.
A fiction, so much of
this spring. The moon
stares numbly down.
Last year's oaks
lassoed by wind. What
feels like the world
will linger then come
to an end. The choco-
late strawberry he
brought oozes thru
plastic untouched
as his tongue or lips.
Only a trace, like the
scent of wintergreen
20 years after my
mother last zipped her
leather bag, still in
the closet of the
house I'm rarely in

WITHOUT
KNOWING THE END

everything that comes
before it has to be
fiction. Still the moon
silhouettes your face.
Of course, that's a lie
too. Only another
would see that and
there's so little time.
The iris tosses its
shadow against the
mirror on the ledge.
Petals drying over
night as love does for
the woman who feels
too tired to leave,
too late to start over

LIKE
A STRESSED TREE
BLOOMING
MORE WILDLY

my hair's grown
down my back these
months. It's an old
story of the daughter
blossoming as the
mother's hair goes
grey. No, that's a
lie. I never wanted
children, only your
skin and my skin
holding me as
it had

I WOULDN'T SAY THE LOST LOVER BRINGS ON RAIN

it's that hole it makes
in Tuesday, leaves you
obsessed with the why.
You lose the cat's
syringe and take the
wrong check book—
the "oh shit" isn't for
the lost barrette,
that you ordered the
wrong size tights
and now it's an extra
trip when you'd rather
just crawl in a quilt
with the cat and shut
out the world where
he still isn't, at least
not for you. If you could
curl into his side,

as if you ever did
you wouldn't swear
at all the manuscript
SASE's that in spite of
more than enough
postage came back
empty and if your
book keeping sucks
like mine, lost forever,
gone. When he isn't
in your life, even
in fantasy, the door to
the metro, closing
just as you rush to make
the train, stands for
everything ahead that
will happen

AM I IN TROUBLE HE ASKS

in a small room,
say a kitchen. The
4 of us are laughing.
"Your reading—it's
that far away," the
one I'm trying to
forget asks. "Let's
storm the café, say
this is Lyn Lifshin,"
and the other tall dark
and handsome picks
up a pizza label and
reads it and it sounds
like it could win any
slam and my lets-
call-him-anything
because he isn't,
really, not to me,
says "yeah, we'll
storm the place, take
over" and I say "maybe
I'll get to read ball
room poems—they
are mostly all I've been
writing and that face,
those eyes, become
deadly serious like
that stare doing a
rumba, leaning into
my eyes as if they were
every part of my body,
as they were every
part of my body in
fantasy. No, as if there
were deeper than anybody's
and he asks "Am I
in trouble now?"

THE CRUSHED, PRESSED WILD PLUM

falling out of my note book
as much a metaphor for
how I fantasized, stupidly.
It went from lipstick blush,
a pale flesh, a scent as musky
as the crevice of a body. Now,
it's flattened and dry too. It's
dead, nothing could revive it.
At least the fantasy sparked
a few good poems. Now
they're shriveled, lifeless,
not even an extended metaphor.
Not even a dream. And what
of the crow that's squawking
wildly at the door to your
studio, a sure sign, always, in
films, of death

BERLIN

I think I've swallowed
the absurd longing
like a cat falling in
love with a dead maple
tree. You know the
story. I throw out the
chocolate he gave me, the
strawberry going bad
like the rest, better in
a poem than in your
mouth a friend said.
She is right. What if
I had put him in my
body. The valium
makes it a relief not
to think tho it will
probably not be as
easy to try to dance
any thought of him
out of me in the ballet
class I'm headed for

WHEN I
THROW OUT
THE COCOLATE
STRAWBERRY

ruined as I thought
everything was
when you dissolved.
When it no longer
looked delicious,
something I was
saving, looking
forward to. When
it was dead, a
dead chocolate, a
dead or lets say
dying who knows
what to call it.
That once sweet.
How you made my
mouth water. Soon
it will make the
refrigerator, what
holds it stink. I should
end here. But then
after I started this
poem he gave more
chocolate, as if
it was his body

THAT SILVER BLUE

at least yours were not
that power blue, color
of blue berries. Another's
had been but he's safely
buried in Arlington,
buried under a flag
while I took a ballet
class. I'm safe (now) from
that tart and sweet, that
feast of dark indigo,
exotic as blue pearls.
I've let go of those rooms,
darkened in late after
noon rain. But these
mahogany eyes, your
eyes, seductive as trains
in the night, moaning,
luring, shiny as polished
chestnuts, bright as
the moon would be if
it was brown or wet bark,
feathered with ebony.
No antidote for them

FAST AS PLUM LACE

snows over old
oak leaves. Not
even the chocolate
covered strawberry
on ice, not even
the arch of the
ache of you. Moon's
sliver wanes. The
geese even louder.
Blood leaves skim
the pond. One pill
helps than the
another. Lately the
one I'm with says
maybe it's you,
you and me, this black-
ness blowing
like a huge tulip.
I feel the petals tug
their shadow
over my mouth

FIRST PAGE
OF A NOTEBOOK

like a heart turned
inside out. Months,
and I think the rain
inside would start
to stop. In rooms
where we slide past
each other, your
hand on mine or
how you look
away paints the
night. And in the
end, none of it
matters. A new note
book, I ought to
turn the page on
you baby but I think
I'm going to need
a few more poems

I REMEMBER THE WOMAN

probably younger than I am
now, dating for the first
time as a widow, marveling
how she didn't feel any
different than she did as a
teen. The waiting for the
phone, wondering, changing
her clothes so many times
before he'd show up,
wondering what it would be
like if he touched her.
Poignant I thought and
chose the piece for a book.
Now even with a man of my
own, fantasies are giving
me insomnia. What to wear
for the next day's class.
Something sweet from Free
People or a little more
sexy? Betsey Johnson or
Bebe? When I can't sleep I
go on line, vowing I won't buy
clothes I don't need as every
thing melts in this economy.
But maybe suede or some
satin mini would bring him to
his knees, a velvet plum
empire lace bodice make
him wild to know what
is underneath. What he
wants, I know, is deeper
in, it's the me he imagines
in books of mine he's
begged for and now has
turned me into. So what
if the covers on the books
aren't current, they're who

I was and that's what he
craves. He'll tire.
A male dancer's life
is done at 40 a Russian teacher
said. But last night when
valium and hot milk didn't
do much, I couldn't
resist checking to see if in his
oxycondon mood he'd
called or e mailed and since
he didn't, and I needed a fix,
I headed for Bebe

WEEK OF NIGHTMARES

In blackness, the cat
leaps thru a screen. I'd
kept gates in front of the
door and she's not even
a kitten, trying to sliver
thru strange holes but
somehow it happened.
It was in the apartment
in VT I no longer have,
my sister's room, the
beige one where she fed
pigeons until the room
filled with lice. My cat,
Jeté, isn't really a jumper
but she leaped down two
floors to the banks of
Otter Creek. Once a
pregnant girl threw her
self against the rocks for
shame of beginning a
baby. There's no time
to think. No back exit

to the water so I dart
half dressed to Main St
to the small road my
mother carried her garbage
to. I'm calling *Jeté, Jeté*
and asking people. If she
used the road she could
run out into the street
and the cars wouldn't see
her, tawny and ticked
or she'd freak and run
into a truck. *Jeté, Jeté.* I'm
hoarse. It happened so
fast but an Aby, who
wouldn't want her. *Baby,*
Baby I'm half singing
across the cars and the
abandoned railroad track.
Soon it would be dark
and the only stars, some
strangers' cigarettes

WHY,
WITH THE READINGS OVER

nightmares of them,
never ending well.
The ones I'm late
for, the ones I lose
the address for,
get there on the
wrong date. Last
night two of the
worst. I went down
to make the cat's
injection, just wrote
"two bad dreams"
on a scrap

DREAM OF MY MOTHER
PICKING UP MY UNCLE
AND BUKOWSKI

and the night before, a tall
literary man, a cross between
the gangling man in ball room
and the lead in Shall we Kiss—
not a looker and not that nice,
just as well that he left early.
I haven't slept well but if
Bukowski is coming, I want to
put my Outsider issues on him
out. It was 5 dollars when I
bought it. I want to scatter the
other books, even the one I
never returned to my ballet
friend Laura. I don't know what
I should wear. What clothes
would Buk want to see, want to
a woman in? Not any, I suppose
but this is a different kind of
visit. A short suede mini?
Jeans? And what on earth will
Buk and my uncle even talk
about? The two in my house at
the same time? And the house is
a mess. I'd been thinking of
taking two ballet classes this
morning but there's no time. Buk's
books, I think some are in another
house six hours away. It's all
all seeming too much, an overdose.

And there are boxes piled all
over the house. At least my mother
is driving to get them. I think of
something I need to tell her
but I don't have a phone and even
if I did I don't have her cell which
I know she didn't have, I don't
know if anyone had when she
was alive and besides even tho
lying half asleep I am certain I
better clean up the house tho they
all, my mother, my uncle and
Buk, are still dead

BASEMENTS

after the wire net,
maybe no more squirrels

but what of the fencing
helmet as much a mesh

as the nightmares of
women he never

lived with. Looney
tunes or lonely tunes

In the cellar, the webs
hold old stories,

under the packed earth
ghosts of those who

painted the rooms but
left the closets

cherry and emerald,
the color of jewels,

something in code

LATE SUMMER
AFTERNOON
ON APPLETREE

dew past 9 AM.
Leaves still shadow,
a jade light, in the
bed near the shutters,
another Aby cat.
How many lovers
listened to the
maple branches
like antlers? How
many nights,
waiting for their
call? Too many. My
mother in the next
room moaning
as I waited for
nurses, waited for
Hospice, didn't know
I'd ever feel
alive again

IT WAS ALWAYS
LATE SUMMER
WHEN HE WAS LEAVING

longer shadows,
first leaf burning wildness

more emerald in
the grass

no more banging
my knuckles to blood

no more blue sweat
shirt man drooped

over the table, smashed.
But still, how he took

me in his arms and
for July I thought my

heart still dancing,
it always would

SO WHEN HE LEFT

I longed for the old
house I had. So often,
late summer in that
house, marigolds
on the steps for a
lost weekend.
One year I raked
maple leaves until
I passed out. The
long shadows,
the long space
where his body
was. Only the hand
print on the wall,
all that there was
of him

IN A CITY OF STRANGERS

sometimes it's a relief
to have it all done,
become code blue,
no mess, no fuss.
Gone like a pilot who
crashes and is never
heard from again.
There and not there
like a cat embryo
absorbed into the
mother cat's blood.
Over, past stains and
longing. Finished as the
poems and relation
ships never are.
Complete. What you
cherished, diamonds,
rubies, all those clothes
that never kept the
blues from the door,
discarded. Those men
like lovers that didn't
call tho they wanted
a piece of you, pieces
of clothes too small
for any of them, the
chance gone, as close to
you as for now
they can get

THE MAD GIRL SEES THE HOMECOMING
OF THE RELEASED YOUNG ASIAN HOSTAGES

flying into the arms of
the ones who adore them,
air borne nearly. It's as
if the arms of those
longing for them
have magnets
in their fingers.
One's young daughter
clasps her, she
could be imagining
she's seen a ghost, mirage,
not her mother for
real. The mother
melts into her husband.
The three, sculpture,
each curve a part of the
whole. What has
been a hole,
whole again. Their
curves, a cove,
shelter, and the other
young woman, her

mother in tears. She can
hardly believe the
moment is true. Tears.
The circle of their
bodies and I am
thinking, too, of another
time I could have been
one of them only
so much of what matters
has been hacked away.
No one calls. Before
the phone was a bullet
ringing, a hack saw.
Once she ached for
silence. There were arms
and mouths, too many,
but they would have
come with tears
and roses and seeing,
the mad girl knows
for her, no one, again
will care that way

THE POEM
I WANTED TO WRITE YOU

would be as crisp and
clean as this mid October
morning. It would be
just as the explosion
of color starts to creep
in. It's cloudless as
what I'm trying to write
could be. In such light,
even the blighted gardens
blatant as what I am
trying to camouflage
glow wildly

WHY I WRITE ON THE METRO

the cat won't throw up
on just printed pages
or a skirt from Bebe
I plan to return. She
wants to nuzzle,
sleep on my note
books, turn words
to fur. I write on
Metro with out a
black berry I won't
be tempted to check
FaceBook or email.
Somewhere else on a
perfect October Day, a
couple walks thru
orange leaves. Let's
call them vermilion
—a word my first
college teacher called
purple, called verboten.

Do they see the colors,
or my focus on the
closeness of skin, each
other's eyes, fingers.
On the metro, no one
talks to me. I can eaves
drop but I won't have
lunch with anybody,
listen to the phone.
I can free flow, be
anonymous, not see
a stain I ought to fix.
I won't be tempted to
lie out in apricot light
or hear the door bell
clang. I won't hear a
tea kettle or opera
blaring in the next
room and then, the
smell burning

251

LIKE A WOUNDED DEER
SLINKING OFF
INTO THE WOODS

gash from his wounds
still dripping. If there
was snow, a blood
trail. I don't want to
talk. You'd think the
scar tissue would make
me numb, tough but
his stags get thru.
I'm not what I used
to be. Sometimes I still
can leap, seem suspended
in air. Sometimes it
doesn't seem
worth escape

THE POEM
I WANTED TO WRITE

would camouflage
pain, hysteria.
It would have the
color of a
fall day, say today,
October 11.
That poem wouldn't
have to hide, un-
typed in drawers
or dress in sequins
or lace or leather to
get you to look.
It would move easily
as a classic fox trot,
show enough to
make you want more
but not enough
to scare you
or my self

AUGUST 24

already the dark moves
in fast. Fireflies settle
in close to earth. Some
thing is about to change.
Years ago, your foot on
the wedding glass, the
guitar in the Daimler.
Later, days flat as photo–
graphs of the ceremony
still in the garage. You
tore your shirt off in a
rage. Buttons spit like
hail. Years later, the
quiet back in upstate
New York, three gray
fox—and yes, like in
fox trot the glide, low
and smooth, a dark
scrim, pearl gray
as memory

OBSESSION

tarnished as when the
words poured out of you

days, onyx as the
blackest horses,
a midnight
without a moon

If I give it a
name, can I
bury it?

Already the days
are getting shorter

Would a plane dropping
from the sky
shatter more?

Would a daughter's
pink skin and long
blonde hair, in love
with the miracle

of soap bubbles,
the glint and shimmer
have pulled the light
in, spit in it out,
the diamonds and rhinestones

DARK NIGHT PURPLE

a deeper, more scarlet
blue blue. Seattle haze
with its mulberry shadow.
You know what I mean,
blue as empty arms and
the blue your baby brought.
Thunder cloud, a gray
lavender blue when the
one you want leaves you. No
blue as blue as that hot
ice rich blue, not school
boy blue, forget nostalgia,
a deep twilight blue or
bell grave victory blue

ON THAT KIND
OF THURSDAY

a rain daze, blue
summer sky, blue
crystalline. Where
you can't see every
thing touches every
thing. Summer splash,
misty afternoon.
My heart of lace
and old tulle. Some
where else the blues-
maker is adjusting
his mask. He knows
his best side and
hardly anyone knows
his words. His lips,
a blur in blue. Deep
blue sea blue.
Cosmic blue, blue
burst mountain lake
blue, bluer than
blue, as later, longing,
when I least expect
his touch makes me

UPSTATE RAIN

this dark rain,
Wednesday afternoon
turning the bedroom
to a leaf dripping
cove. Green's the
only color, the sill,
glass beads too far
from that year you
were captive. The
lights went out late
afternoon, dark with
dark wood ceiling
a cove of rain and
our thighs a skin
bracelet. That long–
ing, electric as the
flashes. I wanted to
freeze what happened
and was happening

slow afternoons in my
grandmother's kitchen
years after the bedroom
of wasps where, terrified,
I couldn't sleep waiting
for my mother to come
back from giving birth.
Later Sundays the grown
ups slapped cards, vowed
no one made brownies
like my grandmother.
I watched under the
stained glass chandelier
thru French glass doors,
drifted into the velvet
painting of women in silk
and gauze moving thru
ebony water under a
silver moon. Life seemed
on hold, even weeks
there getting ready for
my wedding when my
mother moved out of the
apartment, sued my father
for divorce. My black
cat, Othello, lived that
August on the screened
porch as peonies filled
with ants and news came
of Marilyn dying. Later I'd
say I got married to give
my cat a home. Later
the painting on the landing
some early 20th century
itinerant painter turned the
bland walls into a landscape

I imagined I could step
into, was painted over. The
stained glass would disappear
and the conch shell I heard
oceans in and the green
rug that seemed like
the sea. I have the Chinese
chair and a table for cards
in my own house. The art
deco lady glows. Soon
stucco would be torn off walls,
the grandfather clock refuse
to continue. The garden would
go, glass canisters I loved
as a child stay stored in the
cellar of a house I'm rarely in.
The room where my mother
slept when a sick baby, where
her father took the hired girl
and whispered come pussy,
come kitty pussy while
my grandmother tossed,
sleepless upstairs in her own
bed became the room my
uncle, no longer able to climb
stairs, slept with, his new bride:
the oxygen tank, the closest
of all he was tied to. But more
vivid than the houses I've
lived in later, fall afternoons
when I was still the fat kid
in that house of
leaves we tunneled thru,
our special house, like tents
we made of blankets where we
watched fire flies in the night
wet grass, and that snow fortress,
igloos, where cuddled in
blankets near the evergreen

my mother
and grandmother brought hot chocolate
that would never,
anywhere else, taste
as sweet again

SLOW AFTERNOON, MAIN STREET

summers in my uncle's store,
fans hummed but the air stayed
heavy, old. Mornings straightening
the tangled pile of shorts. Airless,
airless. Heels and cinch belts.
Crinolines. Maybe some new boy,
a summer visitor would come
looking for chinos, someone
smelling of horses and hay
looking for bib overalls,
asking if I know his boy. I
dreamt of going to Hollywood,
of fame even snobby Laurie Gibbs
will notice. When it doesn't
rain, when there's no shipment of
new clothes, no boys in from
summer camps, just late afternoon
heat, flies in the distance, day
dreams fragile as a glass
rose, all there was until what
mattered would begin

38 MAIN STREET

those summer afternoons,
Otter Creek close to a trickle

the breeze up from the
old mill. My mother would

pack the car for Branbury Beach.
Salmon croquettes in a

heavy picnic basket. Hot
raspberry sun turned

the lavender room orchid.
My hair still damp

from the lake, my mother
came in with water, rubbed

my back. "It will be ok,"
she whispered rubbing my

back until she couldn't.
That image glows, the sound

of a train, her breathing.
Like bubbles shimmering,

glistening till they dissolve
as if they never were

OH YES THE MARBLE EGGS
AND THE BOOKS ON PARIS

and the Christmas decorations
that somehow no longer
bring that little "that
year" twinge and the
check book stubs that are
like a diary: I am shredding
them. I found and kept
my parents' for years but I
want to shred, I want to
travel light. Sure my garage
in New York is something
else: all the letters my
mother wrote me thru life
and the ones she saved from
me. A box that says "things"
in the lavender bedroom
where I've hardly slept
since college. Then a
canister set from my grand
mother. I wanted it as a child
and now what on earth and
where on earth would I
put it? Like too much
I've left

PURPLE MAN

there on the metro at
Foggy Bottom or
Faragut West. Bright
purple beret, purple
trouser, jacket, a
purple tie print.
Purple handkerchief.
His socks must
be purple too.
Concord grape,
the darkest plums.
I think of the woman
at Garde de Nord,
as purple but more
flamboyant. Big
blond hair and veil,
purple velvet, a
poem about her
probably in some
one's moldy cellar.
I haven't seen it
for years but I see her

so clearly, ordering
one mint tea after
another, waiting in
her purple velvet,
purple and dark orchid
lipstick matching
her nails. Purple, the
color of death,
of mourning. We
were leaving Paris
for Berlin. First I
thought she was waiting
for a date, then I
saw purple fishnet
stockings, how
she cased the crowd
with a constant smile
as if painted on.
Waiting, nothing like
an American hooker,
more like someone in a
Shakespearean play

WILD TO GET YOU OUT OF ANY MORE POEMS

I think of the woman who
threw the mug at Mona
Lisa, how it wasn't the
first time. A rock once,
a cod. And today, in late
summer what was it she
was throwing to get it
out of herself? Rage at
some man? The feeling
her life had not gone as
she expected? She was
not in her senses Paris
police said. Was it Mona
Lisa's serious look on a
day she found maybe
she, or her daughter, had
an incurable disease?
This was summer and did
she imagine a simple
walk thru Tuilleires,
an afternoon drifting
thru flowers, bread and
café au lait under wild
Japonica and then the

news, a bullet, so
unfair when she'd just
got back to wanting to
live again after what
she thought she could
not get thru was past.
The mug, still warm
from the too sweet too
bitter coffee flung
desperately, a rash
act, like smothering
a shrieking child
or finding the one who
mattered had cleared
out his things
that morning. Smug
really, knowing what
she won't reveal,
doesn't have to be
gloating, sneering,
daring her, taunting her
to get whatever was
wild inside her out

THE MAD GIRL
WATCHES THE MAN
WITH HAIR TO CEMENT

right there, on a side
walk bench, not a mirage
of a male Medusa but
there in Silver Spring
with cars and buses
slamming past. More
hair than Rapunzel.
A squirrel, a cat could
follow the river of hair
up his shoulder and
his head. Who knows
what lies in those
curls, what mice or
beetles lust for such a
nest. Who knows why
he seems frozen, a pose
of hair, a hair statue,
a hair trail stretching
across town, a lasso
of darkness, braid
who knows what
could sliver up or
down, escape
what is

ALMOST THE END
OF JULY

on the metro
until the tunnel
it's stifling with
little time to
write. Each
image flaunts
its lips, large
breasts, in a
shocking pink
low cut top
shimmers like
white caps, silver
with onyx horses,
the darkness
of them against
a red sea

WHEN I PASS THE PLACE

where my car slid off the road,
where amethyst barrettes
were flung from bloody hair,
forehead scalped

I'd be late for the film
whined in siren light

And who would tell the
friend I was meeting.
"Stay with us a man with
blue eyes said over

and over. The night
grass, September dew.

My mustang left like
litter. I suppose my
heart took a deep breath,
If there were sparrows

I didn't hear them

OVER
ONE HUNDRED STITCHES

high on horror,

the lilac sweatshirt,
a blood Rorschach

where is it now?
days I didn't want
to wash it, a badge

of the worst and
I'd gotten through

AUGUST, THEN AFTER

I light a candle for
my mother in the
house I'm rarely
in, can see her
lighting one in
the same room
for her mother.
In Vermont, the
geese were already
flying. Skies of
small blackbirds
like tossed coals.
The dark moss
on her stone. So
much in my rear view
mirror now that she
isn't eclipsed.
Other pain. Never
mind what I said
before. When I walked
into the room, just
a glance took
my breath

"NOSTALGIC MEMENTOS"

on the side of the box.
Letters from my mother
in college, room assignments
for Syracuse U. Someone
sprinkled baby talc powder
on the box. Musty files.
A letter from a Carl I
no longer remember, the
ink blurred: "Shaw .5th
floor," UVM *Kake Walk*
magazine before it was
not pc, Feb 16,17, 18.
Those handsome men
probably white and bent.
Xerox copy of a script
spelled wrong, "Rosalin,
Litman" then a photo
of me in the green dress
I wore. Measles couldn't
stop me. I was Vivian
Whitehouse, attractive
young girl about 24.
I probably was, though
younger, with no idea I was
pretty. That part, after
I lost others to Carolyn
Morin who went on to have
an affair with Joe DiMaggio
who came to Middlebury
to make Carolyn's mother,
too, until Mr. Morin went
after him with a shotgun.
The pale ink of the script
fading, crumbling like
those days, blurred as the
handwritten notes under
the powder, messy
as the past

Hotel Lifshin

THE HOTEL LIFSHIN IS CLOSING ITS DOORS

It has to

the guests have
gone downhill,
are gluttons

the head cook is so
frazzled he
lost his wallet

the air hums
with complaints: only 42
types of jam? Why
isn't there more

variety in the coffee?
Nobody thinks of their
rooms as anything

but disposable. The
velvet pillows slammed on
the floor near over

full cups dripping honey.
And the one who flies
helicopters in the

main room, skims
Tiffany lights and heir
loom china, when

after three times I ask
him to stop, beg
desist, doesn't,

aims the helicopter

toward my head

Enough, the guests aren't
what they used to be.
expect food on the hour

One, amazed she didn't
feel well after eating
the food off everyone's
plate, wants the dining

room to be sixty degrees,
shrieks and tears off her
clothes when it hits 61

The butler tries to keep
up, keep a smile but
under the mask he's
unraveling, loses his
keys, his Visa card

Animals miles away
from the hotel hear the
loud yelps and moans
and head for the mountains

Hotel Lifshin has had it with
men trying to get in
to the wrong rooms,

the hotel has done
its best, expected
demands, tried to

fulfil them. But one
wants a clock

275

removed from her
wall. The tick she
says is so loud she

can't sleep tho no
body else can hear
it. She wants a
silver pin, a gold

pin. She wants, maybe
being short, to lord it
over everyone with
her voice. She'll take
your cell phone, your
yogurt dip off your

plate, hide sharp things
under velvet cushions.
And when she's driven

everyone away, she'll
stay out on the balcony,
nude, try to boss the stars

If you come here expecting
the butler to sprint to every
whine, sprint for books, for
clothes of mine that would
never fit any of the guests,
know skis are not here on
demand. Come expecting
a choice of 12 course meals
on the hour. Wreck our room,
steal the prized bathroom
accessories or fly a battery
operated helicopter into
stained Tiffany glass and then
into the Steuben vase, and
you'll be shown the door.

If you come expecting to be
supplied with your own cell
phone, computer, fashionista
clothes and rip them in
seconds or whine about the
food, that you can't adjust
the temperature, steal the
hotel's books and towels and
silver: please don't come.

The Hotel Lifshin is sick
of being servant,
maid, butler, then kicked
around by guests who pay
only for food, forget the
lodgings. The hotel is
exhausted. It's been
overfull, people sleeping
in the main room, the
lobby. Even the ones in
rooms race the stairs in
underwear. No one sane
would want this long
bombardment. These
guests want you to walk
them to the metro and fund
their train and then they
fly toy helicopters into
your heirloom Heywood
Wakefield mirrors and then
snarl "is the coffee ready?"
They bleat at 3 AM, want a
choice of 300 teas the
waiter can never clear the
tables since they eat all
day. They rearrange
the furniture, cram their
suitcases with your specially
saved mementos. And if

she would let them
near, they'd probably
abscond with the cat.

The guests aren't happy,
not even with nanny-like
aid. Whatever the butler
does isn't right, is not
enough. "A pin, an iron,
a metro card, a book,"
one whines. They break
a chair, a mirror, chip
toilet seats and rip the
spread. These guests are
sure everything you do
should be for them. They
sit in the middle of the
lobby floor to use a
computer they help them
selves to. If anyone trips
over them in the dark,
they'll sue.

The Hotel Lifshin
can't keep up,
it can't keep replacing
chests of drawers
the guests gouged.
The hotel can't stand
any more complaints.
If the coffee isn't
there within seconds of
their demands, they
sulk. Rings from
sticky glasses,
indelible on all wood.
Some flying electronic
plane crashes in
to a leaded glass lamp.

The guests sneak
into the kitchen: no
thing is safe. Tiles
crack and there are ruts
in the glass stove.
Coffee pots are in
pieces. Lasagna
is smeared across
the floor. The
velvet doesn't look
like velvet any more,
the furniture can't take it
and neither can the hotel.

Slits in velvet chairs,
ink on the oriental rugs

you won't find the clock
easily, hidden between

sofa cushions because,
the guest says, the

inaudible-to-every-one-else
tick won't let her snore

Of course the blue velvet
will now always have the

shape of the clock in it.

It isn't worth it, exhaustion
bad as a hangover. When
they close the door, the
count of what is missing,
lost, stolen away in cars,
takes up a whole day. It is
not fun. Any unoccupied
room they take for their own

territory, anyone's food
they figure is their own.
"Is coffee made, where are
the cookies, the iron, the
pins, the fudge? Where is
the chocolate, we need
it pronto." As pronto as I
want them out

you can't expect the
butler to bring in and out
the same 12 suitcases
four, maybe five times

you can't expect
someone to clean up
your mess on the hour.
Don't leave towels

and underwear in the
hotel's main room.
How many scratched
tables and stoves,

antique night stands,
forget the smear and
stains on the wall
before you think you

ought to pay? No one in
the hotel can understand
how guests would need to
use to wall to tally up

their Scrabble score.

Over 20 years is enough
the stained carpets,
the noises. The way

the butler can get so
overwhelmed, lose his
wallets. You imagine a
lower main room, or
lobby, a fireplace the
guest can read by
or talk. You imagine
civility, that the
guests know they are
guests and not five year
olds in kindergarten,
plastic fly toys around the
room even tho you've
warned them. And who
needs complaints that
the hotel hasn't left
chocolates on the bed?

The Hotel Lifshin is sick
of the chaos, the
clamor sick of being
asked—there's not a
minute free—how the
showers work, where the
TV remote is and why
one can't work , can't
remember how to get
on his sweater. They
want you to find the
weather report for
them. Want you to
bring coffee and tea.
They want twenty
four hour room service,
would never dream of
leaving a tip.

do you have an iron
and ironing board?

Do you have a pin?
Do you have a different kind
    of bread?
Do you have the weather
    report, the
schedule from trains?
Where are extra towels and
quilts?
Do you have the TV zapper?
Do you have eggs?
Do you have another
    sweater?
Do you have a different
    pan?
Do you have a grater?
Do you have garlic?
Do you have potatoes?
Do you have more wine?
Will you bring it to me?
Do you have real and decaf
    coffee,
30 kinds of jams? Where are
    the
bagels? Where have the fifty
dollars worth of cookies
    gone?
Where is the cat, where
are the glasses. Who can
    find
Jim's wallet? Do you have
some fresh herbs?
    Something
light? It's "do you have"
sixty times on the
hour until the
hotel has
had it.

It's not the taxes, but

gusts with chain saws
in the bathroom sawing
notches on the toilet.
Well, maybe not chain
saws but probably
razors, like teenagers
would their names on
a desk. Gouges on
the bathtubs, towel
racks pulled out of the
wall when the cocoa
isn't the right brand
or the coffee isn't
vanilla. French vanilla.

The Hotel Lifshin has
tried to serve it's guests well,
prepared with a stocked larder,
ice chests for every room,
matching towels and
    comforters
in each closet.

They wanted more. Something
was always missing. They
    took the
hotel's private cell phones,
wore them out, flew birds
thru the lobby, the kitchen.
    The
cook was sure feathers would
land in the stew. Crystals
    shattered,
velvet was torn. The hotel
management smiled and it
    was "hup
to" for the next demand

but it was never enough. Just

chocolates on their pillow
didn't do much: they wanted
chocolate in their boots
and books and undies.

There are rules: anybody
polite would know them.
The hotel has its own
needs tho the guests
don't seem to know it,
playing electronic bass
and accordion all thru the
night. A knock on the
door, a knock on the
ceiling doesn't get thru.
The towels set out
are not for rubbing black
shoe polish on the floor.
The coffee pot is not
a toilet. This is not the
place for 24 hour room
service. We don't welcome
your flying toys buzzing
Tiffany lamp shades.
Please don't complain
there are only seventeen
kinds of jam.

Please do
not open the door when
it's only zero outside
And please don't think
you, as at a real hotel,
can stay from fall to spring.
If you don't like the
sleeping arrangements,
feel free to check out,
find a place on your
own. And please do

not put prized books
under the couch's
bottom so it ruins
not only books but
bends the frame. Would
you be pleased to find
holes in your favorite
books, a hole in the
carpet? Would you do
this in a real hotel?
Would you do it
in your house?

Even if you're on
vacation, this is not
the place to bring
your wild dogs,
even some real
hotels don't allow
it. This is not the
place to barge into
other rooms even
if you'd had a
bad dream. Don't
take 12 bottles
of spring water with
you when you
go for a walk, a
doggy bag for the
road is one thing
but do you think it
is nice to grab,
without asking,
food from an
other's plate?

We have limited capacity,
remember not to lug in
your whole house, laundry